© 2022 Authors

ISBN: 978-83-67405-04-1

DOI: https://doi.org/10.2478/9788367405027

THEORETICAL INTRODUCTION 4
1. **FOOTBALL - DISCIPLINE CHARACTERISTICS** 5
   1.1. Evolution in training 8
2. **FOOTBALL WARM-UP** 11
   2.1. The importance of warming up in preparing the players' bodies 11
   2.2. Factors affecting a warm-up 12
   2.3. Types of warm-ups 13
   2.3.1. Passive warm-up 13
   2.3.2. Active warm-up 14
   2.4. Warm-up methodology (structure and standards) 14
   2.4.1. Warm-up structure 15
   2.5. Warming up before a match (competition) and training (class) 25
   2.6. Types of warm-up organization 25
   2.7. Types of warm-up before classes 27
PRACTICAL EXAMPLES 30
3. **SUGGESTIONS FOR VARIOUS PRE-MATCH WARM-UP RUNS** 30
   3.1. Proposition of a pre-match warm-up 30
   3.2. Pre-match warm-up for the Polish national team in an international friendly match against Slovenia 33
   3.3. Pre-match warm-up of the leading team of the Polish Ekstraklasa - Legia Warsaw 36
   3.4. Pre-match warm-up for the GKS Tychy club in Fortuna I League 39
   3.5. Pre-match warm-up for the GKS Katowice club in Fortuna I League 41
   3.6. Pre-match warm-up of the team of the Polish Ekstraklasa - RKS Radomiak Radom 43
   3.7. Goalkeeper pre-match warm-up proposal 46
   3.8. The goalkeeper warm-up performed before the match of F.C. Barcelona ...
   47
4. **SUGGESTIONS FOR VARIOUS WARM-UP RUNS BEFORE TRAINING AND SCHOOL CLASSES** 50
   4.1. Universal warm-up course before training sessions 50
   4.1.1. Proposition of a general warm-up course without gear 50
   4.1.2. Proposition of a general warm-up course with gear other than a ball 51
   4.1.3. Proposition of a warm-up with a ball 52
   4.1.4. Proposition of a warm-up course with a ball and special technique elements 53
   4.1.5. Proposition of a warm-up course with a ball and tactical elements 54
   4.1.6. Proposition of a combined warm-up (mixed) course 55
   4.1.7. Proposition of a goalkeeper warm-up course 56

5. **SUGGESTIONS FOR TRAINING SETTINGS USED TO WARM-UP** 57
   5.1. Suggestions of training settings that can be used in general development warm-up without accessories 57
   5.2. Suggestions of training settings that can be used in a general development warm-up using equipment other than a ball 62
   5.3. Suggestions of training settings that can be used in a general warm-up with a ball 73
   5.4. Suggestions of training settings that can be used in a focused warm-up with a ball and special technique elements..83
   5.5. Suggestions of training settings that can be used in a warm-up with a ball and elements of tactics 88
6. **WARM-UP SCENARIOS BEFORE TRAINING SESSIONS** 94
   6.1. Scenario of a general warm-up without equipment before training sessions 94
   6.2. Scenario of a general warm-up with equipment other than a ball before training sessions 106
   6.3. Scenario of a general warm-up with a ball before training...................... 115
   6.4. Ball-oriented warm-up scenarios and special technique elements before training sessions 127
   6.5. Scenario of a warm-up with a ball and elements of game tactics before training 136
   6.6. Combined warm-up scenario before training sessions 146
   6.7. Goalkeeper warm-up scenario before training... 158
   BIBLIOGRAPHY 169

THEORETICAL INTRODUCTION

According to researchers Chmura and Jung (1992), Martín-García et al., (2018) modern football sets an ever-increasing amount of expectations on players in terms of technical, tactical, physical and mental preparation.

The effective use of football skills during the game and training depends primarily on excellent psychomotor preparation, high technical and tactical skills, a high tolerance of increasing fatigue, and a properly implemented warm-up (Chmura and Jung 1992, Chmura 2014).

During sporting competitions or football practices, players perform complex and varied activities such as: ball jumps, running at a variable pace (stops and starts), and actions with a ball (kicking, receiving, changing direction, leading, feints). Work with maximum or submaximal load is often performed during a football match or training session. The organism of a professional player and a child starting his or her football adventure should be prepared for such an effort. The above task is completed by the warm-up carried out by the leader (coach) before the match or training. It should always appear in the beginning part of training or classes and precede participation in sporting competitions.

Unfortunately, observing school and club sporting competitions, I regret to say that not all trainers attach sufficient importance on the proper preparation of their players. A competition or practice is often preceded by a five-minute jog around the pitch and several shots on goal. Ignorance about running a warm-up is very dangerous and can lead to many unpleasant consequences, e.g. severe injuries of the youngest players.

The theoretical and scientific aspects of warming up in football were raised by many authors (Bischops and Gerards 1999, Chmura 2014, Bouhlel 2018, Miguel et al. 2018).

However, in most of the publications dealing with the issues of football warm-up, only individual examples of their practical applications have been presented. Conversely, books offered for exercisers do not take into account scientific research and the diverse nature of training (technical, tactical, motor) in the organization of the warm-up (James 2004, Beale 2007, 2015, Sardar and Verma 2014, Friedrich 2015, Gerards 2017).

The main goal of this work is to present the necessary theoretical knowledge and broadly understood practical applications for coaches as well as physical education teachers conducting football classes. The book includes many ready-made football warm-up scenarios, with an emphasis on various training options to exclude monotony.

1. FOOTBALL - DISCIPLINE CHARACTERISTICS

Analysing the authors' claims (Żmuda, Szyngiera, Góralczyk 1999, Wagner, Rumak 2001, Fajfer 2003, Talaga 2006a, Stępiński 2007, Szwarc, Piątek 2010, Czubaj, Drozda, Myszkorowski 2012, Kirkendall 2012), football can be considered a hegemon among all disciplines of sport, and certainly the most widespread game. It is popular among adults as well as children and adolescents. It is difficult to explain this phenomenon and one can only assume that it owes its position to its general availability. Regardless of the conditions and the level of players, it can be played by everyone and almost anywhere. Football is also characterized by an incredible variety of forms of movement and countless combinations in attack and defence. Viewers can watch many football matches without getting tired because of the dynamic nature of the game and its lack of repetition. During the game, a footballer and spectator constantly experience new emotions.

Sports with a multi-stakeholder nature are team sports. Understanding team sports in an ordered praxeological chain is possible thanks to the works of the following authors (Naglak 1994, 2001, Panfil 2006, Szwarc 2003, Duda 2004a, 2008). Multi-subjectivity is characterized by the fact that players' actions are enforced and are distributive, which in turn means that each of them performs separate tasks for a common goal - victory. Players occupy positions that are organized by the tasks they are meant to accomplish and thus perform different functions (Naglak 2001). Team sports are a battle between two groups of athletes, each of which strives to achieve the same goal. The players' task is to achieve the intended result with all available methods and means, within strictly defined rules and regulations (Szwarc 2003).

Playing football allows for the implementation of various elements of physical exercise. However, there is a fundamental difference between playing football, used as a means in physical education, and playing as understood as a discipline. In the first case, the game is modified so that its organization and level of difficulty allows for the active participation of all participants, regardless of their talents, and the adopted forms of activity should act as a stimulator allowing for the most comprehensive development possible, i.e. the game is selected according to the participants' capabilities. In the second case, the situation reverses, and the ball becomes the target. The level of the performance during the game becomes the basis for the selection of players and the means of preparation for competition in football. In this case, selected athletes must meet the requirements of the sport as a discipline (Panfil, Paluszek 2003). The goal of the two teams' fight is to achieve victory using permitted technical and tactical actions. The right of physical contact with an opponent is determined by the rules of the game (Jastrzębski, Szwarc 2003).

Two 11-person teams take up the fight. During the game, they influence each other through two types of group actions - attack and defence (Naglak 2005). These teams, through individual and group efforts of their players, attempt to limit the possibilities of the opponent, whose goal is to win. The main goal of the game in attack is to score a goal, while in a defensive game it is to take the ball away from the opponent in a manner consistent with the rules of the game. The most important element of the situation in the game is the player who, having specific abilities, makes decisions about individual or group actions. Acting in situations, he tries to achieve the goals and tasks of the game (Nosal 1999).

During a football match, players are subject to inter-unit influences regarding the interactions of other persons in visual or auditory contact. The interactions of spectators (coaches, experts and the audience) and teammates can have a positive or negative effect on the activities performed by the player during the game (Panfil 2006).

When describing the game, it should be noted that many exercises used for the preparation of the players are constructed as a result of situations in which they may find themselves during gameplay. In general, the game situation is a balance of power: 11 players on one team and 11 players on the other. Analytically, the player's game situation in the context of rivalry with the opponent boils down to a 1 × 1 balance of power, while in the context of cooperation with a partner while competing with the opponent creates temporary arrangements and advantages of force: 2 × 1. These systems, depending on the phase of the game, place of action, and indirectly, the result and the current time of the game are beneficial, or not, in achieving the goals (Nosal 1999).

The competition often involves a direct duel with a rival which necessitates perfect motor preparation and the ability to act individually, as well as in a team, at the appropriate level. The implementation of complex movement tasks in the game is conditioned by the player's previous actions while learning the basic habits and movement elements specific to the actions in the game. The stronger the reflex-conditioned relationships developed during the learning of individual motor elements, the easier it is to synthesize new forms of movements. When a player performs an action, he applies a specific movement (technical) activity dependant on the constantly changing situation around him. His awareness is focused on the analysis of the situation, on making the most appropriate decisions in hopes of achieving the goals of the game, and on the selection of the most purposeful moves (Duda 2008). The best players in the game must make split second decisions. The following factors influence the correct performance of individual elements during the game: concentration, coordination, motor speed and developed movement habits (Kucharczyk 2013). Football places a high demand not only on the state of physical preparation of the player and his nervous system, but also on the features of his psyche: perception, attention, memory, thinking, imagination, emotions, and volitional and moral features. During the game, the player consciously strives to achieve the intended goal, influencing the decisions made and the specific type of motor activity performed. In this way, he takes an active part in the game, because he makes decisions as to the goals and how to act in a specific situation on the pitch. A footballer must have certain mental predispositions (Figure 1) to be able to make rational decisions based on the goals of the game, bringing forth the intended result (Duda 2004a).

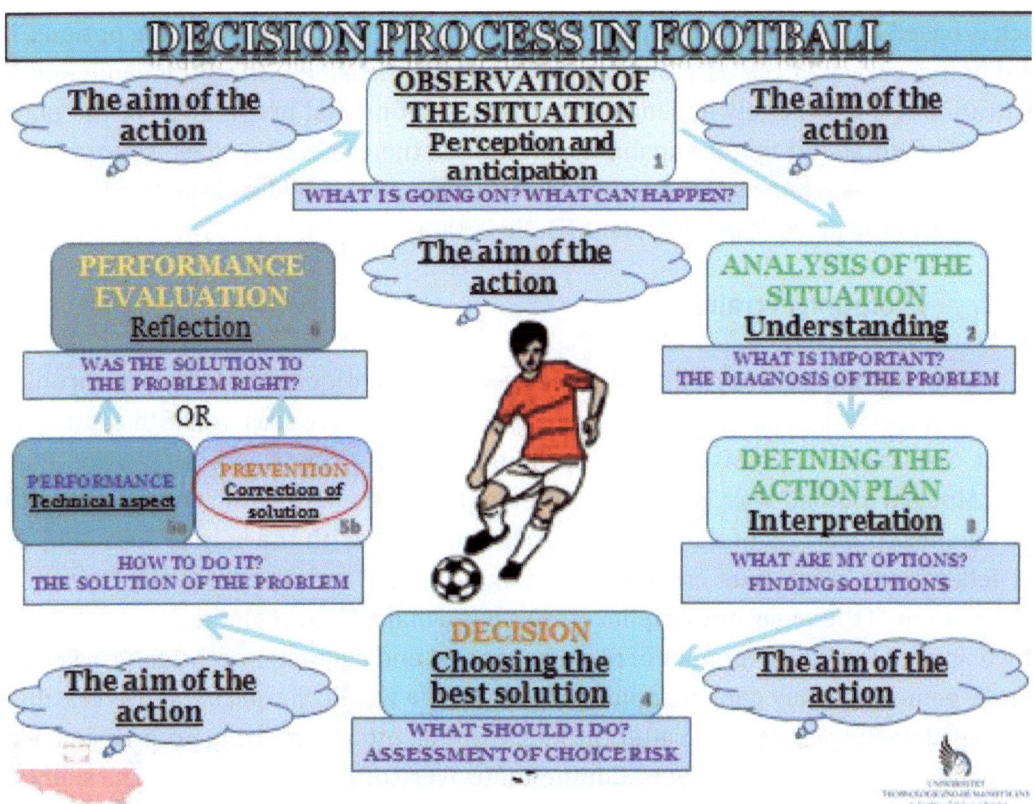

Figure 1. Elements characterizing the player's mental activities (own study based on Duda 2004, 2008, Grycmann and Szyngiera 2016).

A footballer, wanting to perform efficiently in dynamic game situations, should have the ability to predict the consequences of events (anticipation), i.e. the possibility, occurrence or non-existence of any favourable or unfavourable situation in the future. Effective prediction of events depends significantly on the fund of knowledge on how to act in various situations (Duda, Basiaga-Pasternak 2009). After surveying the situation during the game the player makes an assessment, determining the systems formed in time and space. An example would be the distance from the goal, the speed at which their partner and opponent move, and their skills. The time taken to make a decision largely affects the assessment, and its range is very short. The more knowledge and experience the player has, the more rational the assessment. An assessment must always be made before the action (Duda 2004a). Actions at a certain point in the game result from a previously made decision. That is to say, an internal act of a player manifests in the actions of others. Decision making is a continuous process throughout the game. Choosing one course of action entails another. Players during an attack play perform actions with and without the ball. Those on the defence act (counteract) against the player with the ball as well as the players without the ball (Nosal 1999). The speed of decision making and its implementation, adequate to the situation on the field, is related to the player's reaction time. Choosing among multiple possibilities, the player decides his course of action which, in a given situation, he considers to be the best. It is a kind of dynamic decision making, which is based on a disjoint alternative, i.e. the choice between two excluding options, the speed and accuracy of the assessment of the situation arising during the game and the exact rational choice largely dependent on the state of mental preparation of the player, and on his mental and motor capabilities. It seems, therefore, that these factors largely determine the effectiveness of the activities performed on the field and success in teaching at all stages of the player's development (Duda 2004a).

1.1. Evolution in training

The beginnings of various ball games go back to antiquity. Old Chinese chronicles show that imperial soldiers played it as a part of military exercises in the 5th century B.C. Ancient Greeks and Romans also played football, among other sports (Szwarc, Piątek 2010). Modern football was "created" by the English in the late 18th century. The actual separation of supporters of the game took place in 1863, with the help of arms and legs. Two federations were thus created: The Rugby Union and The Football Union. The establishment of the separate disciplines' rules had a major impact on the games' character (dimensions of the fields, number of players, content and character of the game). Football - a "new game" - quickly gained popularity around the world. Simplicity and accessibility encouraged young people to run after the ball, while an often surprising progression of the game gained the interest of viewers. Competitions were often organized and the skill level of players and teams increased (Talaga 2006b). In 1904, the International Football Federation (FIFA) was created, which now cooperates with over 200 national football associations.

According to Talaga (1997), the increase in the popularity of football, as well as the concern for a higher level of play, had a positive impact not only on the further evolution of tactics, but also on the strategy of the game. Conducting an effective match on the pitch requires a proper selection of strategy, as well as imposing a specific style of play on the opponent. The direction of work of representatives who share common views and methods also depends on ethnic conditions, geographical location and football traditions we call game schools. Analyses of football competitions have shown that representatives of major football schools, i.e. European and South American, are trying to maintain their own specificity, while also absorbing the most valuable attributes from their opponents. As a result of deriving positive qualities from both sides, the game becomes more interesting, universal and modern, and the result is always difficult to predict. Stępiński (2009) emphasizes that formations are only graphic shots, modified many times and changed during the game depending on whether the team is attacking or defending. The most commonly used formations are: 1-4-3-3, 1-3-5-2, 1-4-4-2, 1-4-5-1 and 1-4-2-3-1. The genesis of the creation and application of formations, styles and schools has been thoroughly described by Polish experts (Talaga 1997, Żmuda 1998, Panfil, Żmuda 1999, Stępiński 2009, Szwarc, Piątek 2010).

There is no doubt among theoreticians and exercisers of team sports that the results of the analysis of match activity (style and ways of resolving offensive and defensive situations) of the world's leading teams should be used as a guideline for the development of the training program for other teams, including national teams (Wrzos 2005). Modern training must reproduce, to the right extent and scope, the conditions and requirements of a match. This extensive and extremely valuable material (how valuable it is depends on the quality of the analysis) should form the basis of discussions regarding changes to training programs and their adaptation to the current requirements as dictated by the best of various groups and categories of players. And this is followed by the selection of appropriate methods, forms and means of training (Duda 2004b, 2006a).

For over eighty years, participation in the world cup finals has been the number one goal and often crowns the career of every professional player in this sport. Spectacular performances at the World Cup immortalized players such as Pele, Maradona, Euzebio, Beckenbauer and Zidane (Kuczma 2010). Game analysis of the best teams allows for data to be obtained that helps determine the content and forms of the training process. Big football competitions, such as the World or European Championships, also provide a lot of valuable material and are therefore subject to scientific analysis (Stuła 1998, Żmuda 2001, Bergier, Buraczewski 2003, Verheijen 2003, Duda 2006b and others). The pursuit of winning has had a significant impact on the evolution of formations, which currently play a significant role in football tactics. Changes and trends in game tactics have been described by many native and foreign authors (Panfil, Żmuda 1999, Lucchesi 2000, Talaga 2006b, Stępiński 2007, Wilson 2009, Martin 2012 and others).

Football games are assessed by various indicators, their course is also determined by incommensurable factors, such as formations, players 'mental dispositions, interpretation of regulations, referees, playing in weakness and others. The problem boils down to drawing the right conclusions for your training session. In modern high-qualified football, training work cannot be based on intuition and a "coaches nose". There are no ready-made, simple recipes for success, but one can and must, using the results of the analysis presented above, formulate training drills and should strive for what is effective. Practically, this will, in many cases, mean changes in the training program, adaptation of methods with regards to the training objective, change of its organization and conditions, etc. The contemporary football game requires more and more from players in terms of physical, general and special fitness, as well as technical and tactical skills. There is no other way to achieve and maintain a high level of players and team than a well-planned, targeted and systematic training. Making training resemble the ideal game, as well as the individualization of the session are the main conclusions drawn from these studies (Wrzos 2005).

Maybe it is worth realizing that the technique of the game was and will remain the basis for assessing player training, provides freedom of play, and creates the possibility of implementing tactical assumptions. Brazilians stand out in this respect, different from representatives of the Scandinavian school and Englishmen, who put more emphasis on other elements of the game. Polish players underachieve in that respect. Where does it come from? Certainly, the player's technical training is influenced by motor skills, which, to some extent, are genetically determined, such as coordination skills. The method of teaching technique is simultaneously influenced by, and shapes the movement stereotype in young players, later expanding it and consolidating it in adults (Doktór, Talaga, Pilkiewicz 2002).

Football training has evolved along with the tactics of the game, and the effects of the team's work are influenced not only by the coach, but also by a large group of people analysing the progress of the players using specialized research. Players are under the constant care of specialists in the fields of psychology, physiology, motor preparation, biochemistry, wellness and many others. The knowledge of the team of employed experts enables the player to be properly prepared for competition at the highest level. In the largest football clubs they are employed to carry out specific tasks, which includes the proper preparation of players for training and matches with the help of an appropriate warm-up. Unfortunately, in lower-rank clubs, i.e. most clubs in the world, the coach is responsible for all aspects of training. Therefore, he should know an adequate amount of drills and methods of their progression and regression depending on the needs of the players and the nature of the training sessions. Therefore, I decided to divide the warm-up into individual types and kinds that will allow for the easier selection depending on the objectives of the practice. It should also be mentioned that in the age of the Internet, trainers have access to a powerful database of training structures, and warm-up suggestions, but this knowledge is not systematized and named to make the usage easier.

2. FOOTBALL WARM-UP

2.1. The importance of warming up in preparing the players' bodies

According to Chmura (2014), warm-up in modern sports plays an extremely important role. The warm-up consists of specially planned physical exercises, the task of which is to prepare the exercising body for the effort performed during training or competition.

Warming up, through a varied but gradually increasing intensity of exercise, also allows you to soften or completely exclude the appearance of a so-called "blind spot" that often occurs when performing high or medium intensity exercises. Overcoming the blind spot is mainly due to facilitated breathing (the so-called second breath) (Cicirko 2004).

As noted by Kubica (1995) and Chmura (2014), the goal of warming up before a match or training is to:
- take physiological factors from resting to stress in the scope of oxygen supply mechanisms, thermoregulation, energy and electrolyte management as well as the function of internal secretion glands,
- explore the nerve pathways involved in the conduction of impulses associated with the course of conditional reflexes (movement habits), examining the basis for performing a specific motion technique,
- prepare the entire motor apparatus, i.e. muscles, ligaments and joints for the correct and efficient implementation of learned motor habits and to reduce the risk of injury, as well as modify and regulate the influence of emotional pre-game/practice states,
- lead to the optimal stimulation of the central nervous system and to reach the threshold of psychomotor fatigue, as well as the highest efficiency and effectiveness of this system,
- reduce the risk of contusion and injury,
- improve motor coordination, increase the feeling for the ball, as well as the movement, speed and smoothness of its performance,
- improve the player's mental attitude in regard to the implementation of technical and tactical tasks,
- modify and regulate emotional pre-game/practice states.

The impact of warm-up exercises on the body is invaluable, has a multifaceted influence (Chmura 2014) and is associated with the following benefits (Bischops and Gerards 1999, Chmura 2014):
- they cause an increase in body and muscle temperature,
- affect the acceleration of the metabolism,
- increase the efficiency of the central nervous system,
- dynamize effort energy,
- reduce the risk of injury,
- reduce joint loads,
- relieve pre-game/practice tension,

> increase the chance of preventing an opponent from scoring a goal or quickly scoring a goal.

According to the above information, a properly performed warm-up is very important, and therefore, under no circumstances should it be omitted or carried out carelessly.

I support the opinion of Chmura (2014), which states that a poorly warmed up player has a problem with entering the match (in its early stages), is unable to fully use his potential (psychomotor and effort, as well as technical and tactical skills), and has problems with creativity during the game. The player then makes many simple technical and tactical mistakes by making wrong decisions during the game. According to the study (Abade et al. 2017, Hammami et al. 2018) warming up again after a 15-minute break allows you to get into the second half better and avoid injury.

Warming up is a must, not only before a competition, but also before each training session. Only when properly carried out can you achieve your fullest potential. And it doesn't matter if it comes before an important Champions League match or before a school training. Let the scientific research supporting this thesis be its confirmation.

2.2. Factors affecting a warm-up

Quoting Bischops and Gerards 1999, Chmura 2014, it should be noted that there are many factors affecting the intensity and composition of the warm-up before a class and match. It should include:

> <u>warm-up intensity (players' training status)</u> - the greater the players' training status, the greater the warm-up intensity should be. However, when warming up, it should be remembered to apply loads of gradually increasing intensity, not short bouts of high intensity, which causes a slow increase in body temperature. The individual threshold of psychomotor fatigue is also important here, which should be achieved in the warm-up by gradually increasing the exercise load. This means that during warm-up the player should achieve higher values of lactate concentration and heart rate than the values appearing on the lactate threshold of $4 \text{ mmol} \cdot l^{-1}$.

> <u>players age</u> – a regular and planned warm-up is important at all ages, but absolutely necessary from the age of twelve and up. Among younger children, its conduct should be implemented in the form of play and lead to initial adaptation with the help of various types of exercises (most often performed with the ball).

> <u>warm-up duration and external factors that can affect the warm-up</u> - warm-up should last 35-40 minutes (10 minutes in the locker room, gym and about 25-30 minutes on the pitch). The time to warm up before training, depending on the nature of the training, should be 25 to 30 minutes (8-10 minutes in the locker room, gym). Warming up before the match should last from 35-40 minutes (about 10 minutes in the cloakroom, gym). For players to achieve full preparation before training or a match, they must acclimatize to a variety of external conditions, i.e. pitch, audience, time of day, atmospheric conditions (wind, rain, snow or ambient

temperature and humidity), etc. For example, warm-up at high ambient temperatures (25-30°C) and high humidity should last from 20-25 minutes. For speed type athletes and extroverts, it should be 20 minutes, and 25 minutes for endurance type and introverts. At low ambient temperatures (4-5°C or even below freezing) it takes more time to warm up the whole body. It should last from 25-30 minutes for extroverts and speed type and 30 minutes and longer for introverts and endurance type.

➢ <u>choice of warm-up exercises before training and a match</u> - the selection of exercises necessary to warm up should take into account the principles of their usefulness and ease of implementation. It is necessary for the exercises to have a physiological effect and be associated with the specificity of the game. The pre-match warm-up usually follows the same pattern and the exercises are fairly standard. The selection of exercises in a significant part of the warm-up is the same for the whole team, differences appear in the elements preparing the player to play in his position. Exercises carried out in the warm-up before training should be diverse and creative and focused on a specific teaching purpose (the nature of the main part).

➢ <u>individualization of physical loads in the warm-up before training and a match</u> - the selection of training loads (the principle of individualization) should take into account the differences between players in morphological, metabolic and neurophysiological terms. Based on these differences, we can distinguish four types of players with different motor predispositions (types: speed, endurance, endurance-speed with an emphasis on speed and endurance-speed with an emphasis on endurance). The level of stimulation of the central nervous system (CNS), which each player achieves at different stages of warm-up, is caused by the diversity of the team, where there are players with weak and strong nervous systems (introverts and extroverts). Differences in the selection of load individualization may be due to other reasons, i.e. players with injuries, inferior football skills, smaller range of movement, weaker coordination after exceeding 30 years of age or reserve players before the match.

2.3. Types of warm-ups

2.3.1. Passive warm-up

The available literature (Bischops and Gerards 1999, Chmura 2014) distinguishes between two types of warm-up: active and passive (Figure 2). Passive warm-up is carried out by using various forms of warming up the body and muscles, i.e. massages, warm baths and visits to a sauna, showers in hot and cold water, electrostimulation, as well as pharmacological and other means. Of course, this kind of warm-up only has a supporting function and is not able to prepare the player properly for training and match requirements. However, it supplements the active forms of warm-up and offers relaxation to the athlete.

2.3.2. Active warm-up

Active warm-up requires personal commitment and great determination from the player when performing exercises affecting the preparation of the whole body and muscles, the purpose of which is to prepare the player properly for training and matches. In the implementation of active warm-up, the following types are specified (Figure 2): pre-match warm-up and pre-workout warm-up, which can be divided further depending on the nature of the workout.

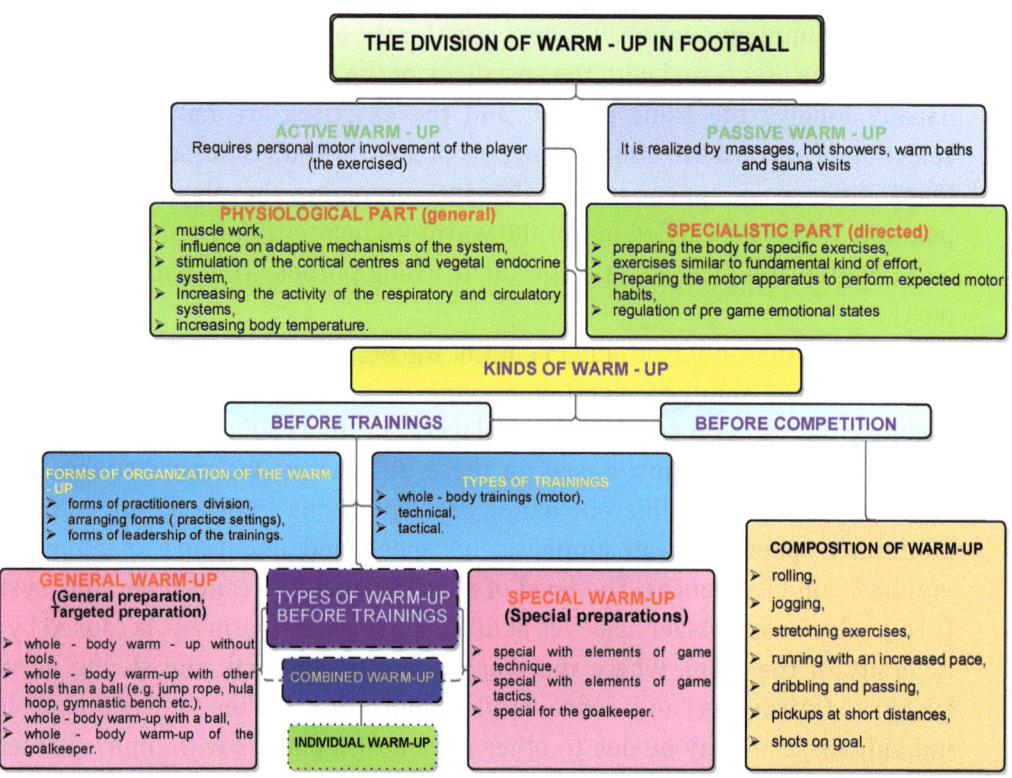

Figure 2. Division of warm-up in football (source - own study based on Talaga 2008).

2.4. Warm-up methodology (structure and standards)

Warm-up methodology is constantly evolving and changing to match current training trends. Many football federations and clubs around the world employ motor preparation specialists to prepare their players for football matches and practices. Unfortunately, there are also many trainers conducting classes who do not appreciate the value of the warm-up, routinely using exercises not necessarily adjusted to the actual needs of training, lessons or competitions.

2.4.1. Warm-up structure

There are many structures (schemes) for warming up. I will try to introduce different concepts of warm-ups before a match or practice proposed by different authors. The type of warm-up should be adapted to the activity it is preceding, a different structure should be planned before a competition than that carried out before classes. The warm-up also varies depending on the purpose for which it is used. Different intensities accompany the classes in which we teach the technique of the game as opposed to the exercises during which we focus on the tactics of the game or implement a training unit with a motoric accent (of speed, strength, explosive strength). Competitions, however, require complete physical and mental fitness from the first minute of the match, so the program must be different from the warm-up program before classes. The pre-competition warm-up is intended to prepare the body for the most intense sports rivalry, while during classes, the participants do not always exercise at ttheir maximum capacity, and so the warm-ups differ from each other.

According to Gołaszewski (2003), Żak and Duda (2008), active warm-up before training usually consists of two parts: general and specialized, which complement each other. The task of the general (warm-up) part is to prepare the player's body for work thanks to a specially selected set of exercises that will increase the efficiency of muscles and joints, increase body temperature, stimulate the circulatory system and prepare the player mentally (nervous and vegetative system) for the tasks ahead. However, the second part of the warm-up (specialized) is related to a specific sport and is designed to prepare the body to perform exercises that are similar to the main part of training and are specific to football.

According to Bischops and Gerards 1999, apart from the general and special parts, it should also be enriched with an individual part (warm-up), which complements the previous two parts (Table 1). In Table 1, the authors attempted to present the main goals of the individual warm-up and ways to achieve them. However, they also point out that it usually does not follow a strict plan. Its individual stages can overlap each other, thus creating a program that an experienced footballer can adapt to his current needs.

The general and specialized parts fulfil the roles that I have mentioned earlier. The individual part (warm-up) is addressed to individual players or small groups (player formation). According to the authors, the necessity of its implementation depends on many different factors, making it is impossible to clearly define a rigid time frame and content, which, in every instance, is determined by a specific factor, e.g. improvement of individual weaknesses, injury, etc.

An interesting proposal of a warm up in football is the FIFA 11+ injury prevention program, which was developed by the international group of FIFA 11+ experts in 2006 and was continued as "The 11 program. Implementation of the FIFA 11+ football warm up program: how to approach and convince the Football associations to invest in prevention."

Table 1. The structure of the warm-up before training and a match according to Bischops and Gerards (Bischops and Gerards 1999).

WARM-UP STRUCTURE		
MAIN OBJECTIVES		**IMPLEMENTATION**
➢ stimulation of the heart and circulatory system ➢ increase body temperature ➢ warming up large groups ➢ preparation for psychological burdens ➢ preparation of the muscular system (strength, stretching, endurance, coordination)	**GENERAL WARM-UP (10 – 15 minutes)**	➢ light jogging and running ➢ exercises engaging the whole body ➢ coordination exercises ➢ stretching exercises to stabilize the motor apparatus ➢ strengthening particularly strained muscles ➢ speed exercises
➢ preparation of the muscular and nervous system to the specific requirements of a given sport discipline (technique, tactics, coordination, endurance, strength) ➢ optimization of mental state	**SPECIAL WARM-UP (10 – 15 minutes)**	➢ dynamic coordination exercises to develop optimal cooperation between muscles and nerves ➢ special preparation for situations in the game
➢ improving individual weaknesses ➢ force regeneration after injuries and longer breaks in the game ➢ taking into account the state of fitness	**INDIVIDUAL WARM-UP**	➢ stretching of contracted muscles ➢ strengthening of weak muscles ➢ special requirements and tasks set during the game

It is intended mainly for amateur or recreational players and is a complete warm-up and preventative program that significantly reduces the risk of injury, which is confirmed by numerous studies (Barengo et al. 2014, Bizzini et al. 2013, 2014, Grooms et al. 2013, Impellizzeri et al. 2013, Meneses-Echávez et al. 2014, Owoeye et al. 2014, Silvers et al. 2015, Rössler et al. 2019). The warm-up course consists of three parts (the first - exercises performed while running, the second - strength, plyometrics, balance, and the third - exercises performed while running) containing 15 exercises in a specific order.

The program was created to be implemented during practices and should be performed at the beginning of each training session, at least twice a week (Steffen, Emery, Romiti, Kang, Bizzini, Dvorak, Finch, Meeuwisse 2013). Using a FIFA 11+ warm-up before a football match is not ideal because its structure lacks specialized exercises with the ball. Preparation for the match requires the use of technical and tactical exercises implemented in various forms, including starting position, passing, receiving, dribbling, and shooting. Thanks to this, players will have time to get used to the ball, as well as the opportunity to adapt to the prevailing conditions. Therefore, the ideal solution would be to create such a pre-match warm-up protocol, in which, in addition to preventive exercises, there will be football exercises. So there seems to be a necessity to create new protocols within the FIFA 11+ model, which can be used before the match and training. The protocols for these warm-ups should take into account the objectives of the classes, which will vary depending on the individual training periods implemented in the structures of the microcycle, mesocycle and macrocycle.

A completely innovative approach in designing the warm-up structure (Table 3) applied by Chmura (2014), based on previous research and scientific work, resulted in a warm-up for team sports, with a focus on football. He divided the warm-up into three phases (local, general and specific) and six stages (two stages in each phase). In each phase, players perform different tasks, using different means and forms that have a different purpose. They form an inseparable whole of preparing the body for effort and each of them is subordinated to the next.

The local phase begins the warm-up program and its main purpose is to warm up the muscles, first by concentric exercises and then by eccentric lower limb exercises. The first two stages are carried out independently by the players in the gym, cloakroom, or playground and must be done before the general warm-up phase begins (first stage - concentric exercises, second stage - eccentric exercises). The main goal of the general warm-up phase is to increase the internal body temperature by activating the respiratory, circulatory and energy systems. During this warm-up phase, the central nervous system is also gradually activated. During the third stage, exercises increasing range of motion are mainly implemented (introductory exercises with or without balls, general improvement exercises, dynamic and static stretching exercises and strengthening exercises adjusted to the individual needs of the players). In the fourth stage, we improve fluidity and increase freedom of movement by performing coordination exercises. They prepare the central and peripheral nervous system, as well as the muscular system to perform the specific movements required for playing football. The specific warm-up phase is the most intense and longest phase in the whole warm-up. During the implementation of this phase, the athlete must achieve his maximum level of intensity in the areas of: neurophysiological, physiological and technical-tactical. The main goal of this phase is to prepare the body for the specific requirements of playing football thanks to stages five and six (stage five - specific exercises with balls, stage six - explosive exercises, specific without balls). These include improving technical and tactical skills, obtaining the best internal body temperature for exercise, stimulating the maximum number of motor units and achieving the level of intensity at which the threshold of psychomotor fatigue appears. The fifth stage contains typical football exercises affecting the players' special technique, e.g. striking (passes, shots), dribbling (feints, driving, body play), ball reception, each taking into account the specificity of the position of the players through the implementation of game fragments, fixed game fragments and small games. This is the longest stage of all stages included in the structure of a football warm-up. Conversely, the sixth stage is the shortest, during which we perform a few seconds of explosive exercises characteristic of playing football and necessary for the perfect stimulation of the CNS (central nervous system) and activating the largest possible number of motor units.

Table 2. Warm-up structure before a FIFA 11+ training.

WARM-UP STRUCTURE FIFA 11+		
PART 1 RUNNING EXERCISES - 8 MINUTES		
1. **RUNNING** STRAIGHT AHEAD	2. **RUNNING** HIP ROTATIONS OUT	3. **RUNNING** HIP ROTATIONS IN
4. **RUNNING** CIRCLING PARTNER	5.**RUNNING** SHOULDER CONTACT	6. **RUNNING** QUICKLY FORWARDS & BACKWARDS
PART 2 STRENGTH · PLYOMETRICS · BALANCE - 10 MINUTES		
7. PLANK	8. SIDEWAYS PLANK	9. HAMSTRINGS
10. SINGLE-LEG STANCE	11. SQUATS	12. JUMPING

PART 3 RUNNING EXERCISES - 2 MINUTES		
13. **RUNNING** ACROSS THE PITCH	14. **RUNNING** BOUNDING	15. **RUNNING** PLANT & CUT

Table 3. Warm-up structure before training and match according to Chmura (Chmura 2014).

WARM-UP STRUCTURE					
STAGE 1			STAGE 2		
Increasing muscle temperature through concentric exercises.		LOCAL PHASE (8-10 minutes) PT (9-11 minutes) PM	Increasing muscle temperature through eccentric exercises.	
Before Training	Before the match		Before training	Before the match
(4 – 5 minutes)	(5 – 6 minutes)		(4 – 5 minutes)	(4 – 5 minutes)
STAGE 3			STAGE 4		
Increasing the range of motion in the joints by dynamic stretching exercises.		GENERAL PHASE (7-10 minutes) PT (9-11 minutes) PM	Increasing fluidity and freedom of movement through coordination exercises.	
Before Training	Before the match		Before training	Before the match
(4 – 6 minutes)	(5 – 6 minutes)		(3 – 4 minutes)	(4 – 5 minutes)
STAGE 5			STAGE 6		
Improving technical and tactical skills through specific exercises with the ball.		SPECIFIC PHASE (7-11 minutes) PT (13-15 minutes) PM	Increasing central nervous system stimulation through explosive exercises.	
Before Training	Before the match		Before training	Before the match
(5 – 8 minutes)	(10 – 11 minutes)		(2 – 3 minutes)	(3 – 4 minutes)

The structure of the pre-match warm-up as described by some authors does not differ from that conducted before practice (Bischops and Gerards 1999). Others (Żak and Duda 2008, Chmura 2014) differentiate the body's preparation for training and match performance, e.g. by the uneven duration of individual warm-up phases (table 3). According to the Chmura (2004) study, a player's pre-match warm-up should be individual, taking into account the intensity and duration of the load used because each player has a different level of arousal at which he works most effectively. Therefore, the warm-up time for each player should be different (with a similar or approximate level of arousal).

This is perfectly reflected in the quote by Maria Nurowska, which says that "everyone is different and that's exciting", therefore, according to Chmura (2004) in footballers with various excitability, warm-ups should be shorter or longer accordingly. He also describes that personality is not always considered by trainers when setting up a training plan, and in many cases is even neglected. Numerous scientific studies indicate that athletes work most efficiently and effectively with optimal stimulation of the nervous system. The level of arousal (Chmura 2014) e.g. too low or too high (examples below for Chmura 2004), negatively affects both the course of training and competition.

The first example
The under stimulated footballer does not distinguish between significant and insignificant moves of the opponent or partner, thus receiving too much stimuli at one time. To process them, he needs a lot of time, which delays his decision-making process (passive play, slow game pace, low goalkeeper's performance).

The second example
The optimally excited football player perceives opponent or teammate's moves that are relevant in a given situation. Therefore, less information flows into the nervous system to be processed, resulting in more time for good and effective implementation of his decision making (for the optimal execution of the selected movement).

The third example
An over-excited footballer does not notice stimuli important for effective play, makes wrong decisions and loses many opportunities (e.g. he takes a shot when he is covered by two defenders, instead of passing the ball to a partner in a free position within a few meters of the goal).

That is why it is important to carry out the optimal warm-up for all players taking into account their personal predispositions.

Analysing the preparation for training and football matches, it should be stated that the warm-up design used by most coaches is based on the structure developed on the basis of many years of European football observations by Loy (2004), which consists of six components:
1. Slow running.
2. Stretching exercises.

3. High-speed running.
4. Dribbling and passing.
5. Short distance sprints.
6. Simple shooting practice.

As part of the individual components, the following exercises were used:

1. Slow running:
- jogging,
- running combined with various forms of jumps,
- running backwards and sideways,
- jogging with arm rotations forwards and backwards.

2. Various stretching exercises:
- anterior and posterior thigh muscles,
- calf muscles.

3. High-speed running:
- runs with graduating intensity over various distances,
- variable intensity running, sometimes faster, sometimes slower.

4. Dribbling and passing:
- dribbling at different paces,
- small games in groups of 2 or 3 players.

5. Short distance sprints:
- sprints for 10 to 15 meters with or without a ball.

6. Simple shooting exercises:
- shots on goal from different positions,
- shots on goal with the ball passed in by the coach (Loy 2004).

Thanks to many years of research, among others by Loya (2004), Kubica (1995), Tyki (1995), Chmura and co-authors (1994, 1998), methodical and practical guidelines have been created that will allow for the development of a warm-up with the least amount of errors:

1. In most of the studied cases, it was found that the warm-up was not directed at the specificity of the position of the player. So, the defenders did not make a single header, the middle midfielders did not make a single cross, and the attackers did not shoot on goal. Therefore, warm-up programs must include the position in which the player plays.
2. Many performed warm-ups do not correspond to the specifics of the game. Shots are taken on goal with a stationary ball outside of the penalty area, when it is known that most shots during the game are taken in the penalty area with a moving

ball. Passes and receptions are usually carried out standing instead of moving. There was a complete lack of such important technical and tactical elements as: crosses while running, headers in offensive and defensive play, head passes, high-speed dribbling etc. Therefore, the warm-up must consider the specificity of football.

3. Apart from shots on goal, all other technical and tactical actions are not directed at the zone in which they occur. They were carried out in completely different areas of the playing field, e.g. long passes were made through the centre of the field, instead of passing the ball diagonally onto the wings. Important technical and tactical elements that constantly appear in the game cannot be completely overlooked.
4. There is no preparation for gameplay situations against opponents. Performing individual actions as a part of warming up without an interfering player leads to the players being unable to quickly switch and achieve the correct rhythm of the game - especially in its initial phase - due to the disruptive actions of the opponent. This is particularly evident when the field of play is condensed and opponents provide a lot of pressure.
5. In the warm-up programs, defensive actions are completely omitted, e.g. no dribbling player is introduced, long passes are not exchanged, etc. Therefore, the warm-up must also take into account defensive requirements.
6. Tactical team activities are also omitted. There are no situations resembling those that occur during the game in which individual players must make quick and deliberate actions. It is rare to practice certain elements that occur in the game. This fact indicates that football warm-up programs must prepare for tactical situations that often occur during actual play.
7. Not enough time is spent stretching, especially leg muscles. Insufficient preparation of the leg muscles for the conditions of the game is one of the main reasons for the occurrence of football injuries. A portion of the warm-up should be focused on stretching as it increases the amplitude of movement in individual joints. It provides an optimally long acceleration path and mitigates muscle injury occurring due to reduction in running speed under the influence of antagonistic muscles. Stretching is important in injury prevention, because the better prepared the muscle and ligament apparatus is for specific loads, the more extensively a given movement can be performed, thus creating a lower risk of injury, e.g. rupture of muscle tendons and joint damage, etc. Therefore, these types of exercises should find a permanent place, not only in each warm-up, but also throughout the training session.
8. Taking into account the contemporary style of football, the warm-up should also include sprinting exercises over very short distances at 2-4-6 meters as well as systematic increases in intensity.
9. Research from Tyka (1995) shows that the best warm-up effect is achieved when we use exercises with an intensity of about 50% VO2max. The research of Chmura and co-authors (1993) showed that players (III and II league) reached their highest

levels of psychomotor efficiency and highest level of endurance exercise at 76% VO2max - which exceeds the threshold intensity by more than 20% (anaerobic transformation threshold).

10. Regarding heart rate (HR), 50-70% HR max. is assumed to be the most effective exercise load during warm-up. A study by Chmura and co-authors (1993) showed that, while performing exercises of increasing intensity, highest psychomotor efficiency and peak central nervous system function occurred at different heart rates, between 152 and 176 beats per minute.

11. Warm-up time in football has a fairly wide time frame and ranges from 10 to 25, and even up to 30 minutes. It depends on the intensity of the exercises, the humidity and ambient temperature of the environment, as well as the level of training of the given player. The author's experience shows that warm-up should last until optimal central nervous system stimulation is achieved, and even this condition should be exceeded. Achieving such a state depends, among other things, on the type of the system and the level of training of the player. Observation of goalkeepers is particularly important, as it concerns not only achieving optimal stimulation of the nervous system just before the start of the match but maintaining it throughout the game. Here often lies the answer to the question why, with a clear advantage in the game by a given team, a quick counterattack by the opponent leads to an unsuccessful intervention by the goalkeeper and ultimately a goal. This is, among other things, the effect of reduced stimulation of the nervous system. This example shows that many possibilities exist in the training of goalkeepers. Numerous studies by Chmura and co-authors (1993) show that competitors with a low level of psychomotor response (slow response) at rest require a longer warm-up with higher intensities, while those with a high-level response (quick response) require a shorter, lower intensity warm-up. The interpretation of the presented research fully confirms this observation, providing further proof for the individualisation of the warm-up. It should be remembered that warm-ups that are too long and intense cause fatigue and reduce the ability of reaching maximum levels of exertion during the match. In light of the facts presented, it is unacceptable to put players into the game after only a short warm-up.

12. The interval between the end of warm-up and the start of the match should not exceed 15-20 minutes. It should be remembered that the later the player starts the game after the warm-up, the less effective it is, because the excitation of the nervous system decreases. Therefore, it is recommended for the player to exceed his optimal level of stimulation of the central nervous system during warm-up, which may allow for the optimal level of stimulation to be reached while waiting for the start of the match. During breaks, an elevated body temperature should be maintained, which can be achieved by using a warm sports outfit.

13. The warm-up must provide the player with an increase in body temperature and accelerate the delivery process of the necessary energy to the muscles.

14. An important criterion during warm-up is achieving an optimal internal body temperature of about 38 degrees Celsius, with a simultaneous muscle temperature of 39 degrees Celsius (1995). Therefore, the effect of overheating the body during warm-up is unacceptable, as it leads, among other things, to dehydration and loss of electrolytes, and, as a consequence, reduction of exercise capacity (Chmura 1999).

A less scientific but no less interesting approach by Bischops and Gerards (1999) on running a warm-up and presentation of mistakes to avoid:
1. Jogging, running and stretching are examples of necessary warm-up exercises.
2. The warm-up is constructed according to a specific pattern and it is not recommended to do high intensity exercises at the beginning.
3. Aspects that will be present later in the training may be introduced in the warm-up (e.g. similarity of exercises).
4. Selected exercises should be mastered as much as possible by all competitors.
5. Coordination exercises should be carried out contralaterally (e.g. left arm, right leg).
6. Competitors should know the goal of the exercises because it increases their motivation.
7. Stretching exercises should be performed before "cold" muscles are strengthened.
8. Each competitor must be able to determine the degree of their own load resistance.
9. During the warm-up, the trainer should work according to a simple method of showing and imitating.
10. As much as possible, the following exercises should be avoided: uncontrolled head rotations, excessive neck loads, excessive loads due to leverage (with legs straightened), explosive movements immediately after stretching, and loads on the knees with their flexion less than 90 degrees (e.g. Cossack dance in a deep squat).

The most common errors during warm-up:
1. Just as reaching high speeds too quickly can cause permanent damage to the engine, so can too forceful warm-up lead to premature exhaustion during the match.
2. During a quick warm-up, the necessary body temperature is not reached, because the human body needs time to receive and process physiological and psychological stimuli.
3. If the warm-up, especially in the part corresponding to the specificity of a given sport discipline, is not adjusted to the assumed requirements, achieving the goal may be difficult or limited (Bischops and Gerards 1999).

In summation, it can be said that contrary to appearances, it is not easy to perform a proper warm-up. It is necessary to know a number of factors that affect the proper preparation of the body for the upcoming exertion. Each trainer knows his team best and knows what exercises and intensity level to use. Considering all of the previously mentioned facts regarding the proper preparation of the body for training and matches, the author of this text decided to present possible settings for running a warm-up, as well as various football warm-up suggestions taking into account the nature of the training sessions. This work will also present the warm-up of teams at various levels in Poland and Europe.

2.5. Warming up before a match (competition) and training (class)

A great deal of determination and commitment is required from the player during the implementation of the warm up program. The main goal of a warm-up is to prepare the body for effort using coordination, stretching, technical and tactical, and explosive exercises, with or without balls. The warm-up should be modified according to the type of exercise it precedes, i.e. a match, training or individual work with the mentee. The differences are that before training the athlete is not accompanied by pre-game emotional states. Therefore, the difference is usually in duration and can be about 10 minutes shorter before training (but does not have to be).

2.6. Types of warm-up organization

Trainings require the trainer to implement a variety of organizational solutions. Knowledge of basic order forms, how to conduct exercises and methods of division of exercisers, as well as their comprehensive use in everyday practice, is the basis for success in the implementation of specific tasks and goals of the teaching process and improvement of football.

The structure of conducting classes is based on specific ways of organizing exercises, carrying out specific movement tasks, relating to the proper use of time and space, as well as maintaining safety during classes. The effectiveness and efficiency of the training process depends, among other things, on the proper selection and use of basic organizational forms.

Figures 3 and 4 below show the possible division of types of warm-up organization, taking into account the range of possibilities of training settings, as well as the division of exercisers and the way of conducting the exercise.

Figure 3. Types of warm-up organization.

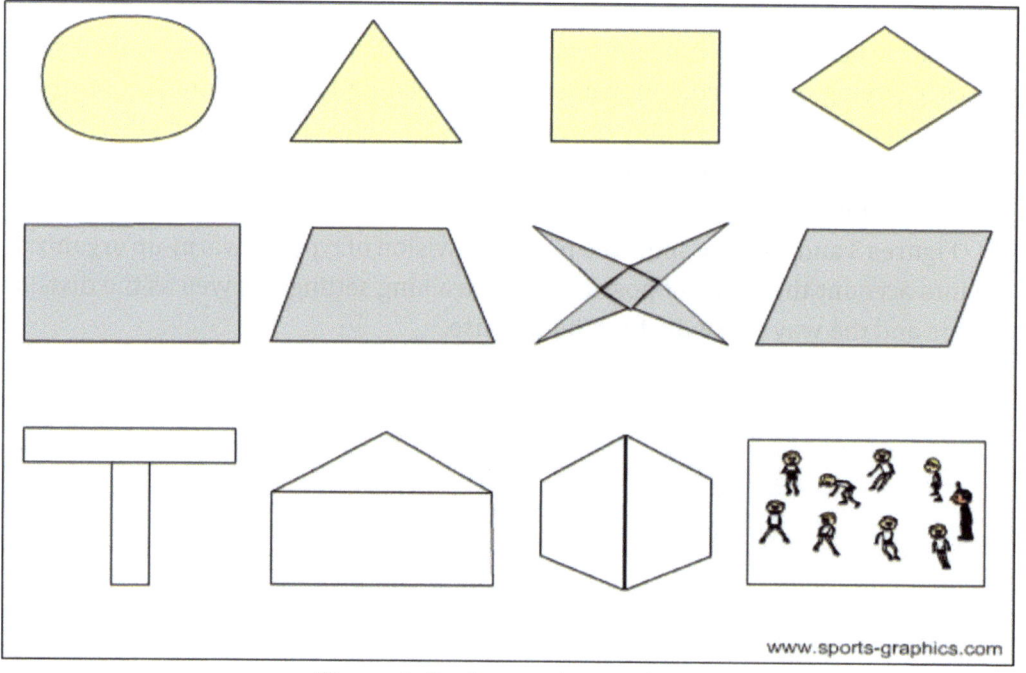

Figure 4. Basic exercise settings.

2.7. Types of warm-up before classes

The figures below (5-9) present the original propositions of the division of different types of warm - ups before classes taking into consideration general, targeted and special preparation.

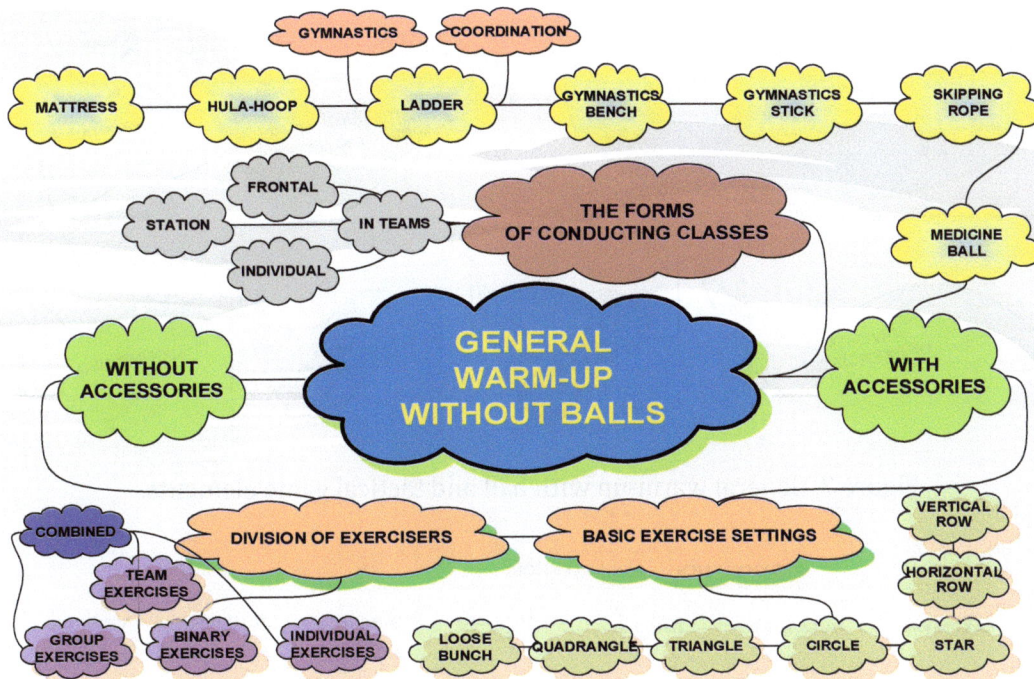

Figure 5. General warm-up without balls – with or without accessories.

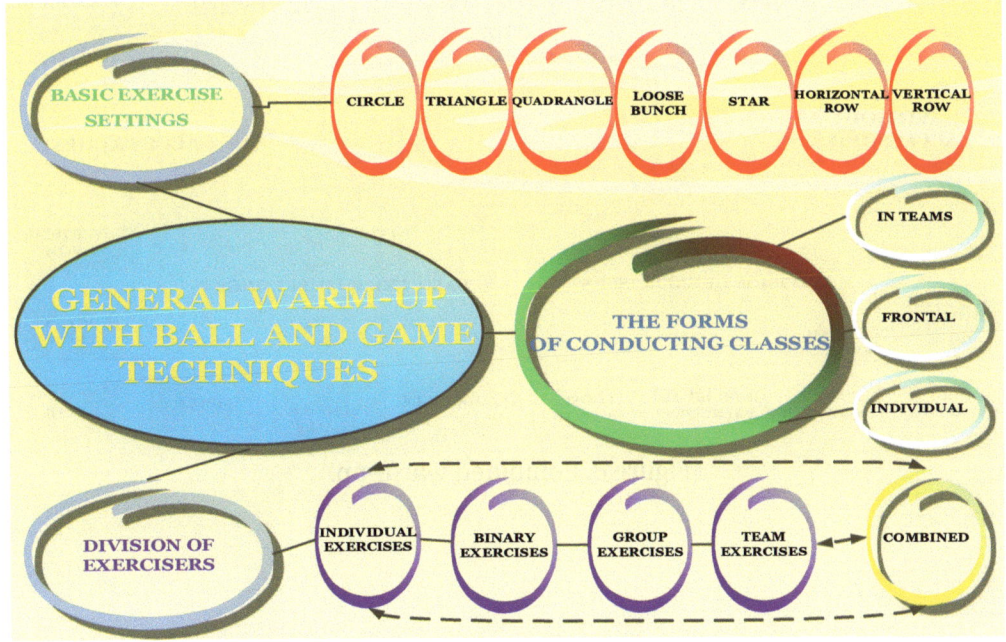

Figure 6. General warm-up with ball and game techniques.

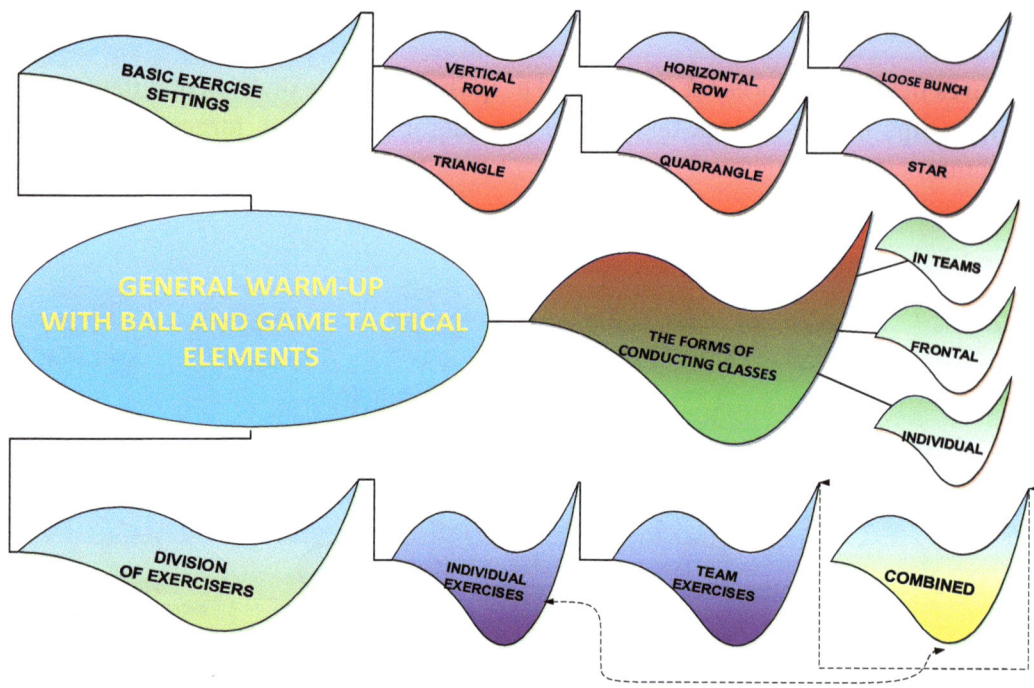

Figure 7. General warm-up with ball and tactical game elements.

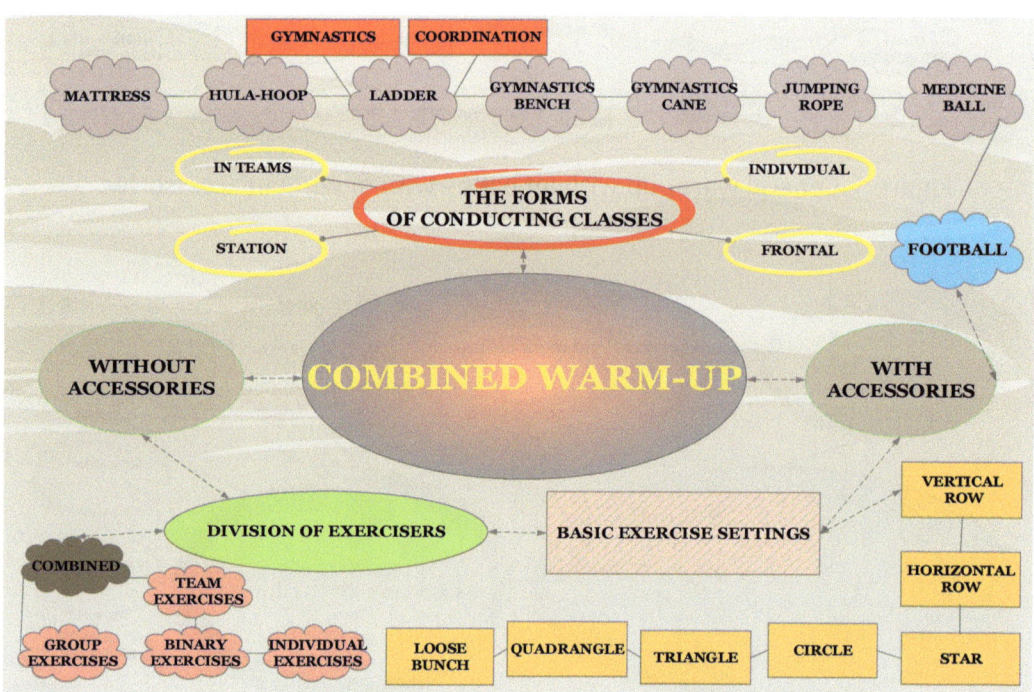

Figure 8. Combined warm-up.

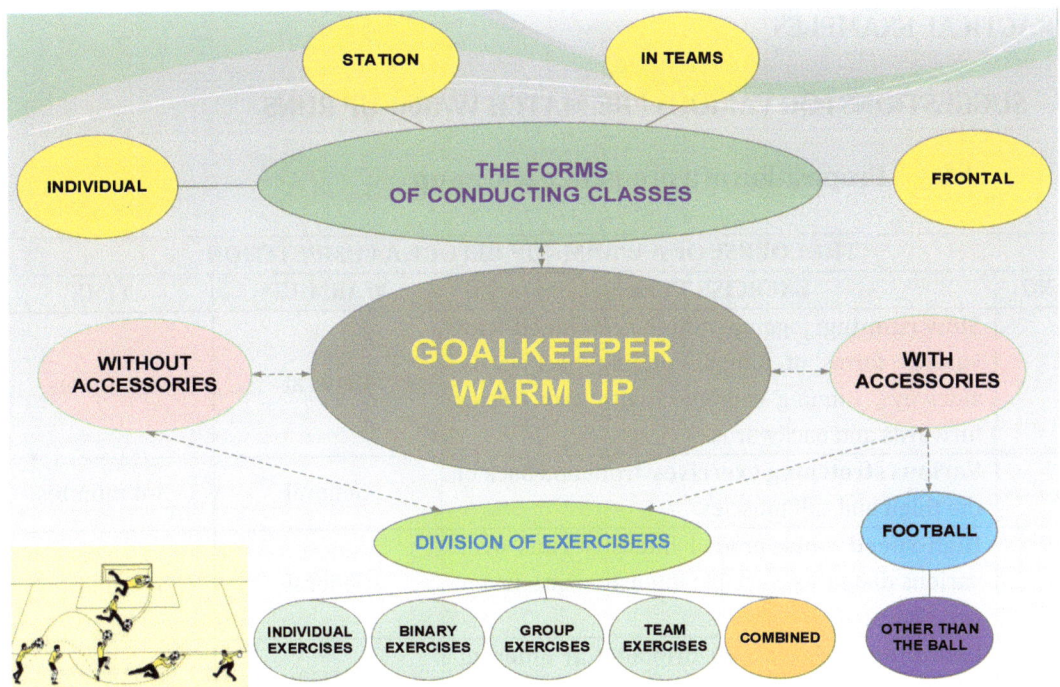

Figure 9. Goalkeeper warm-up.

PRACTICAL EXAMPLES

3. SUGGESTIONS FOR VARIOUS PRE-MATCH WARM-UP RUNS

3.1. Proposition of a pre-match warm-up

THE COURSE OF A WARM - UP BEFORE A COMPETITION			
NO.	EXERCISE TYPE	WARM-UP	TIME
1.	**Slow running:** jogging, running combined with various forms of jumps, running backwards, sideways, running combined with arm circles forwards and backwards.	General	4 minutes
2.	**Various stretching exercises:** front and back of the thigh and calf muscles.	General	3-4 minutes
3.	**High-speed runs:** graded intensity runs over various distances, variable intensity runs, faster and slower.	General	3-4 minutes
4.	**Dribbling and passing:** dribbling at different speeds, small games in groups of 2 or 3 players.	Special	4-5 minutes
5.	**Sprints at short distances:** sprints at 10 to 15 metres without a ball, sprints at 10 to 15 meters with a ball.	Special	4-5 minutes
6.	**Simple shots on goal practice:** shots on goal from different positions, shots on goal with the ball passed in by the coach.	Special	7-8 minutes
	DURATION		25-30 Minutes

OWN STUDY BASED ON LOY'S GUIDELINES (Loy 2000) – DURATION [33']		
DRILLS	EXERCISE SETTING	TIME
I. GENERAL PART **A) Slow run:** a) exercises performed jogging using the coordination ladder and hula hoop with an emphasis on coordination, b) running combined with various forms of jumps, c) running backward and sideways, d) running with arm circles forwards, backwards.	Figure 10. Slow running.	4'
B) Various stretching exercises: a) static stretching exercises with an emphasis on leg muscles (quadriceps, two-headed thighs and calf muscles),		4'

b) dynamic stretching exercises in a team with an emphasis on leg muscles (quadriceps, two-headed thighs and calf muscles).

C) High-speed runs:
a) runs with graduated intensity over various distances,
b) racing with variable intensity runs, once faster, once slower.

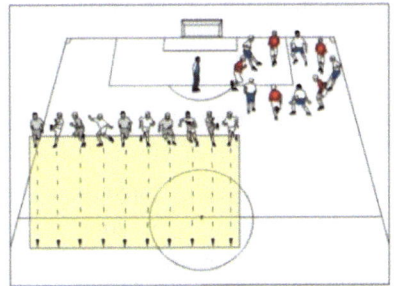

Figure 11. Various stretching exercises.

Figure 12. High-speed running.

4'

II. MAIN PART WITH BALLS
A) Dribbling and passing (outnumbered):
a) dribbling performed at different paces in a small 1x1 game (defender – striker, offensive midfielder - defensive midfielder),
b) 2x2 game plus 1 neutral player playing with the ball on the pitch with dimensions of 15/15 metres. In this game, we care about keeping the ball playing smoothly. One neutral players has the task of helping them keep possession of the ball for as long as possible. If the pressuring team has a problem recovering the ball, the players change at the signal of the coach. Those who are in possession of the ball are supposed to use their numerical advantage and make as many passes as possible. Depending on the players' disposition on a given day max. 2 touch passes, preferably 1. Play two games. The

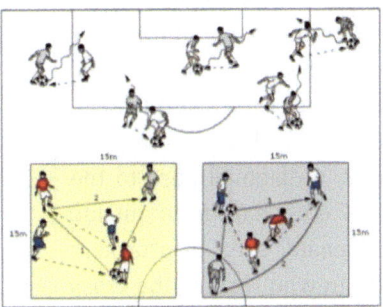

Figure 13. Dribbling and passing.

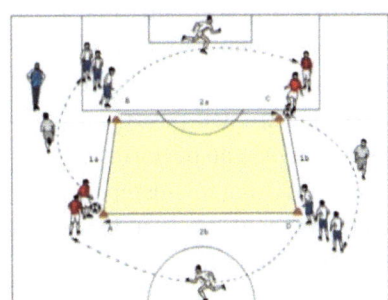

Figure 14. Short sprints without a ball.

7'

first game - 2' (1' active rest – each player performs individual stretching exercises). The second game – 2', [5'].

B) Sprints at short distances:
a) sprints over a distance of 10 to 15 meters without a ball, players placed in a quadrangle in four groups, after passing the ball with the inner part of the foot to the partner, the passing player runs to the next group, the players practice with two balls simultaneously.
b) sprints over a distance of 10 to 15 meters with the ball, players set in a quadrangle in four groups, move to the next group leading the ball as quickly as possible, preferably with a simple and external touch, players practice with four balls simultaneously.

6'

Figure 15. Short sprints with a ball.

III. FINAL PART
Exercises with a shot on goal:
a) left and right wing midfielders and defenders, at centre line level; central defenders, midfielders, and forwards – 1, 5 pass into the centre, 2, 6 diagonal pass to the wing, 3, 7 cross balls from outside of the penalty area to attackers running in who receive the cross and attempt a shot into the sides of the goal,
b) players positioned in two groups, one at the height of the centre line and the other about 30 meters from the goal – 1 perpendicular pass; 2 pass back; 3 half-pass to an incoming partner who performs a one-touch shot using the instep; 4 headshots on goal from a ball thrown in by the coach.

8'

Figure 16. Exercise with a shot on goal after the cross.

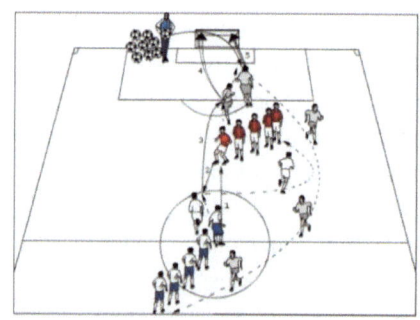
Figure 17. Exercise with a shot on goal after assisting from a partner and throw from the trainer.

3.2. Pre-match warm-up for the Polish national team in an international friendly match against Slovenia

<u>MATERIAL PROVIDED BY THE ADMISSION OF THE CONTEMPORARY SELECTOR OF THE REPRESENTATION OF POLAND ADAM NAWAŁKA AND A TRAINING TEAM.</u>

POLAND AGAINST SLOVENIA ON NOVEMBER 14, 2016 IN WROCŁAW – DURATION [37']		
DRILLS	**EXERCISE SETTING**	**TIME**
I. GENERAL PART **A)** Individual warm-up in the locker room according to the individual needs of the players (flat footwear, available accessories: mats, resistance bands, rollers, bicycles etc.) - a personal trainer is available to competitors. **B)** Preparation for going out to warm up (changing shoes). **C)** Going out to warm up.		3' 3'
II. MAIN PART (on the field) **A)** Passing with a partner (players selected according to positions 2-7, 3-4, 5-11, 6-8, 9-10). **B)** Running and stretching warm-up (physical preparation), trainer. **C)** Passing the ball in two groups of five. **D)** Passing the ball in groups of five along the perimeter with an attack on the player with the ball and support (leg work) – 2x30". Five players outside, five inside in a compact arrangement. After a pass by a player on the perimeter, an attack is made on the player with the ball, the others "cut off" the other players from the passes and support each other. After several repetitions, the teams change roles.	Figure 18. Passing the ball in twos. Figure 19. Running and stretching warm-up.	2' 3' 3' 1'

E) An auxiliary game 5x5 + 2 neutral players on the perimeter - 3x30 "(fluid refill).
The players keep possession of the ball with the help of the two neutral players. After the ball is taken over by the opposing team, they support each other with the neutral players. Six reserve players act as neutral players (two in each of three games).

F) Long passes with a partner (2-7, 3-4, 5-11, 6-8, 9-10).

G) Playing a positional attack ending with a shot on goal.
Variant 1.
The middle midfielders exchange passes with each other, after a few passes one of them makes a diagonal pass to the side defender, who exchanges the pass with the wingman and crosses the ball to two running strikers (before they make a cross change), one of them shoots on the goal, then one of coaches from behind the end line of the pitch gives one more ball for a second shot; possibility of a third ball from the coach in the middle of the pitch. The exercise is executed alternately to the left and to the right. After six passes, players change positions, i.e. numbers VI and VIII change with numbers III and IV (Roman numerals in the figure indicate the numbering of individual players in the game system according to the initial setting).
Variant 2.
The central midfielders make passes in the form of a "crown" with side defenders and continue playing as above.

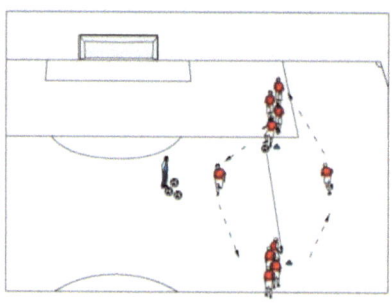
Figure 20. Passing the ball in two groups of five.

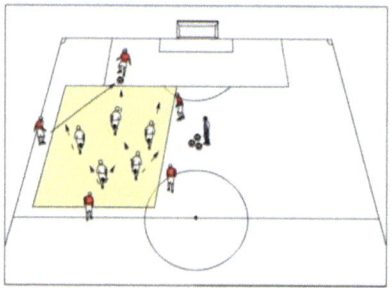
Figure 21. Passing the ball in groups of five along the perimeter with an attack on the player with the ball and support.

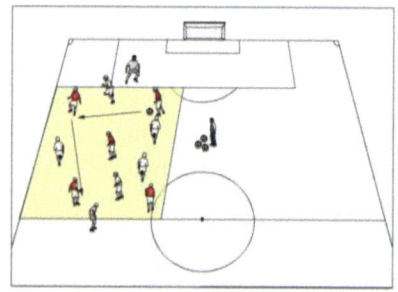
Figure 22. An auxiliary game 5x5 + 2 players neutral on the perimeter.

2'

2'

4'

H) Division into two groups (players from offensive and defensive positions): a) offensive players - shots on goal (16, 20m) The player passes the ball to one of the reserve players, who returns a one-touch pass, then dribbles the ball ending with a shot on goal, after the shot one of the coaches passes the ball on the ground and the player takes a shot (or throws the ball and the player takes a shot with his head). b) defensive players - defensive block cooperation exercise. Variant 1. Players set up in the defence formation, after a pass from the coach, the nearest player attacks the ball, the other defenders move in formation and support the player who left the zone. Competitors from the starting squad perform this exercise alternately with reserve players. Variant 2. The coach passes the ball to one of the central defenders.	 Figure 23. Long-pass balls in pairs. 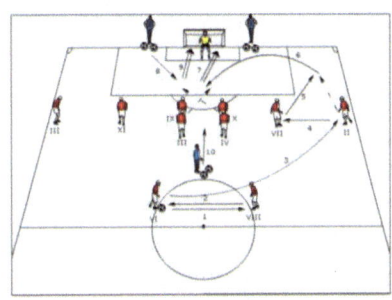 Figure 24. Playing a positional attack ended with a shot on goal. 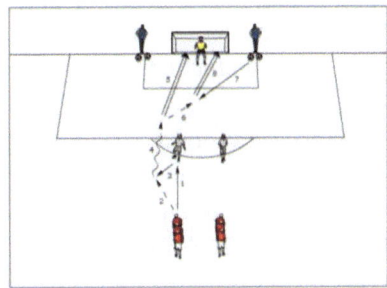 Figure 25. Shots on goal (16, 20m). 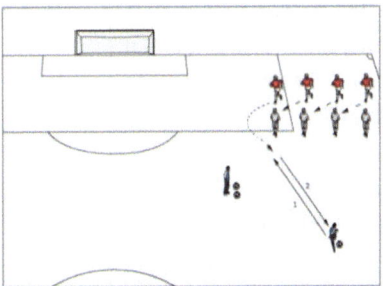 Figure 26. Defence block cooperation exercise.	6' 1' 7'
I) Setup in two queues (10 m - 2 x start, stimulation of central nervous system by the explosive exercises and runaway to the cloakroom).		
J) Last preparations for going out (refilling liquids, massages, etc.).		

| | Noteworthy is the involvement of players not in the starting line-up. These players act as neutral players in the game, pass the ball to the players shooting on the goal or take part in the exercise with players from defensive positions. | | |

3.3. Pre-match warm-up of the leading team of the Polish Ekstraklasa - Legia Warsaw

PREPARED ON THE BASIS OF TALAGA (Talaga 2009) – DURATION [26']		
DRILLS	EXERCISE SETTING	TIME
I. GENERAL PART **A) Running and stretching exercises.** a) jogging and exercises of biceps muscles of the thigh and hip flexors in the form of skipping, b) triple diagonal run three times, loosely, freely, jogging during break, c) stretching exercises, combined with static exercises (leg rotations, abductions, adductions), d) run with three accelerations of 3 metres on the leader's signal.	Figure 27. Exercises running – gym, general development without the ball.	5'
B) Exercises with balls – players matched in pairs (1 ball per pair). a) passing the ball on the ground, leading the ball – passing from a partner - any pass, b) applications for 1-2 touches – a distance of about 10 metres from each other, c) 20-30-meter passes, d) at a distance of 6 meters from each other – playing a thrown ball by a partner – the inner part of the foot, laces, head / 5 times per leg – then switch.	Figure 28. Exercises with the ball in partners.	4'

II. MAIN PART WITH BALLS

A) Numerical advantage for ball possession.

A 4x4 game plus 2 neutral players playing with the ball on a field sized 30/20 meters. In this game, we care about keeping the ball playing smoothly. Two neutral players have the task of helping them keep possession of the ball for as long as possible. If the pressuring team has a problem regaining the ball, the players change at the signal of the coach. Those who own the ball are supposed to use their numerical advantage and maximize the field of play. We pay attention to the accuracy and strength of the passes.

Assumptions of the pressuring players: play close together, attack the player possessing the ball with the use of good timing and strategy – no slide tackles or aggressive play.

The assumptions of „Jokers" is to not leave the centre of the designated field.

All players constantly moving – after playing the ball, skilfully opening up to passes.

Number of touches – having the ball max. 3 touches - „Joker" max. 2 touches.

Team compositions:
1st team – 4 defenders,
2 team – 4 offensive players,
„Jokers" – central midfielders – quarterback.

The first game – 2'30" (1'30" active rest – stretching),

The second game – 2' (1' active rest – stretching).

B) A 6x6 game on half of the pitch.

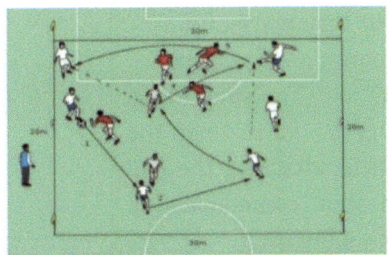

Figure 29. Numerical advantage – 4x4 plus 2 neutral.

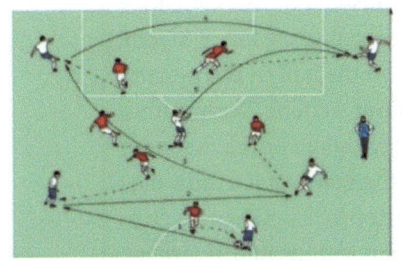

Figure 30. Game of maintenance – 6x6 on half of the field.

7'

4'

	A game with all tactical rules on half of the pitch to introduce players to match conditions – full concentration of players: a) defenders – supporting, shortening / narrowing the playing field, attacking the ball and opponent, communication in defence, footwork, b) midfielders / forwards – quick passes changing the orientation of the game from one side to the other, finishing the action with a shot on goal, crossing, a strong attack on the ball in the penalty area. Four actions lasting until the shot is taken or the defender steals the ball (each action max 30"). After each action, return to starting positions and 15" rest.		
III.	**FINAL PART** **A) Exercises with a shot on goal.** a) side midfielder and defender on the right, b) left midfielder and defender on the left, c) at the height of the penalty area, centre defenders, midfielders, striker – crossing the ball from the side of the field into the penalty area to the attackers (one player after receiving the „cross" definitely attacks the ball heading for the closer post - cross and head hits [duration – 2'], on the ground for a shot[duration – 1']. **B) Sprints for reaction time.** Two 5m sprints and one 16m sprint interspersed with two-headed high flexing exercises and stimulating or relaxing exercises.	 Figure 31. Exercise with a shot on goal. 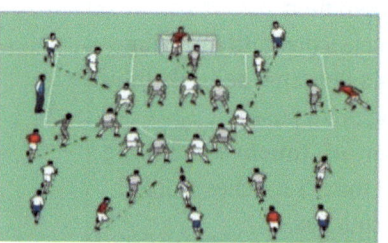 Figure 32. Exercise for speed of reaction time and flexibility.	3' 3'

3.4. Pre-match warm-up for the GKS Tychy club in Fortuna I League

<u>MATERIAL AVAILABLE WITH THE CONSENT OF THE GKS TYCHY CLUB TRAINING TEAM.</u>

AN EXAMPLE OF THE MOST OFTEN USED PRE-MATCH WARM-UP FOR THE GKS TYCHY CLUB IN FORTUNA I LEAGUE IN THE AUTUMN SEASON OF 2019/2020 - DURATION [30']		
DRILLS	EXERCISE SETTING	TIME
I. GENERAL PART Individual warm-up in the locker room, where competitors implement individual programs based on the results of preventive (functional) tests conducted cyclically by the coaching staff.		15'
II. MAIN PART (on the field) **A)** Passes in partners. **B)** Running - stretching warm-up without or with football elements: - running and gym warm-up without balls, - warm-up with football elements. The players perform various exercises in pairs (further away from each other) such as: passing the ball with their feet on the ground using 2-touches, passing using 1-touch, leading the ball towards the partner and performing the feint in front of him with changing places, leading the ball with changing the direction and passing the ball to a friend, quick lead of the ball to the place of the partner with changing places, etc. - running warm-up with football elements. The players perform various exercises in pairs (closer to each other) such as: throwing the ball to the partner with both hands,	Figure 33. Passes in partners. Figure 34. Running and gym warm-up without balls.	2' 6'

passing the ball to the partner with the thigh and playing with the inside of the foot, throwing the ball to the ball with the chest and playing with the leg, throw on the head while standing or with a jump. After completing the exercise, the competitors perform a run of increasing intensity in any direction.

C) Auxiliary game 4x4+2 neutral players – 3' (1", 45", 30").
The players keep possession of the ball with two neutral players. After the ball is taken over by the opposing team, they support each other with neutral players.

D) Scheme of playing the ball in a comprehensive exercise (players in their positions).
The coach passes the ball to one of the central defenders, one of them passes the ball to a player on the wing, where the player's play pattern is applied, e.g. running the ball and crossing to player II (Roman numerals in the figure indicate the numbering of individual players in the game system according to the initial setting), player No. II passing the ball to the player No. VII (the wingman converging earlier from the side sector of the pitch inwards) and playing to the side defender, player No. VII dribbling the ball along the wing and crossing to the incoming attackers (before they perform the "cross change "). After the middle defender makes a diagonal pass, the coach throws the ball at his head (the middle defender runs out and plays the ball to the coach), while the second middle

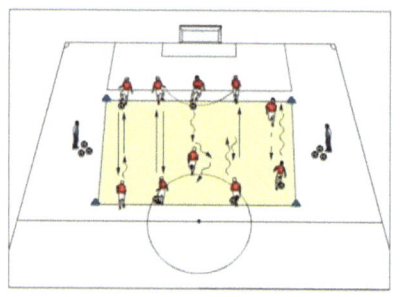

Figure 35. Warm-up with football elements.

3'

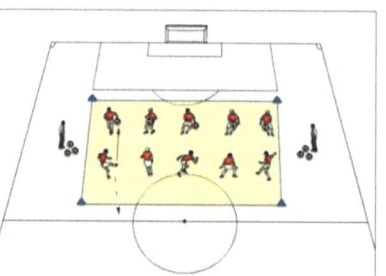

Figure 36. Warm-up with football elements.

5'

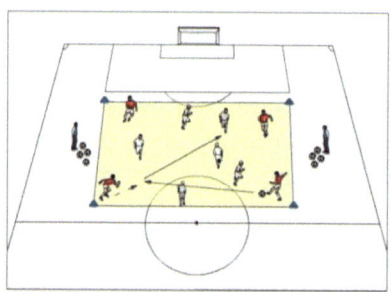

Figure 37. Auxiliary game 4x4 + 2 neutral players.

Figure 38. Scheme of playing the ball in a comprehensive exercise.

defender supports the defensive teammate by placing himself in line with him. The players perform four repetitions, followed by a change in the roles of the players (i.e. players from positions IV and V change with players VI and VIII). E) Shots on goal in two groups. The players alternately pass the ball to the coach, who plays the ball back and after a short dribble the player shoots on goal going to the queue on the other side. F) Splitting into two queues opposite each other (running with a change of direction with running to the side - stimulation of central nervous system, then after a few repetitions run down to the changing room). Depending on the various circumstances concerning each match, the warm-up time can be shortened or extended.	Figure 39. Shots on goal in two groups.	3' 2'

3.5. Pre-match warm-up for the GKS Katowice club in Fortuna I League

<u>MATERIAL AVAILABLE WITH THE CONSENT OF THE GKS KATOWICE CLUB TRAINING TEAM.</u>

PRE-MATCH WARM-UP FOR GKS KATOWICE TEAM IN THE 16TH ROUND OF THE 2ND LEAGUE WITH THE STAL STALOWA WOLA TEAM ON NOVEMBER 2, 2019 AT 6pm – DURATION [32']		
DRILLS	EXERCISE SETTING	TIME
A) Passes in partners. B) Passing the ball in partners combined with dynamic exercises without the ball. The players pass the ball to the partner across from them, and then perform dynamic exercises in place.		2' 8'

C) Running warm-up - placing competitors in a queue, running a distance of 40m twice for 80% of competitors' ability.
D) Group exercise with an emphasis on ball passes and reception.
5 players on the perimeter of the field and 5 in the middle of the field. On the coach's signal, players in the middle perform 4-5 accelerations with a change of direction with the ball (each one has the ball) and play the ball to a player outside of the designated field. After that, they change thier roles.
E) Auxiliary game 4x4 + 2 neutral players on the circuit - 4 '(2x 1'30").
The players keep possession of the ball with two neutral players. After the ball is stolen by the opposing team, they support each other with neutral players.
F) Scheme of playing the ball in a comprehensive exercise (players in their positions).
a) One of the middle defenders passes the ball to the side defender or winger (they change places at their discretion), after receiving the ball he dribbles it (or makes a pass to the winger who plays the defender into the open space) and crosses it into the penalty area to the attackers (previously they perform a cross shift), one of them shoots on goal.
b) Then one of the middle defenders passes the ball to player No. VI or VIII (Roman numerals in the figure indicate the numbering of individual players in the game system

Figure 40. Passes in partners.

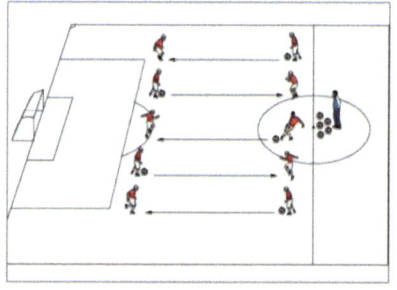

Figure 41. Passing the ball in pairs combined with dynamic exercises without the ball.

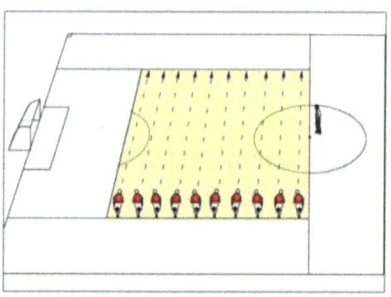

Figure 42. Running warm-up.

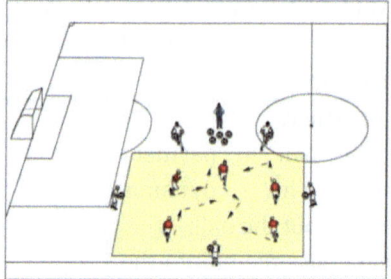

Figure 43. Group exercise with an emphasis on ball passes and receiving.

| 2' |
| 3' |
| 4' |
| 6' |

according to the initial setting), at the command "time" he receives the ball and passes it to one of the attackers, who shoot the ball from the top of the penalty box. In the case of the "back" command, player VI or VIII plays the ball to the defender and he passes it to the player IX or X who shoots on goal.

G) Shots on goal in two groups (2x left leg, 2x right leg).
The players alternately pass the ball to the coach, play the ball and after a short dribble the player shoots on goal and goes to the queue on the other side.

H) Set up in two queues (1x10m, 1x15m, 1x20m, stimulation of central nervous system and runaway to the cloakroom).

The warm-up time is 35 minutes. Reserve players help during the exercises and separately participate in the 6x2 helper game.

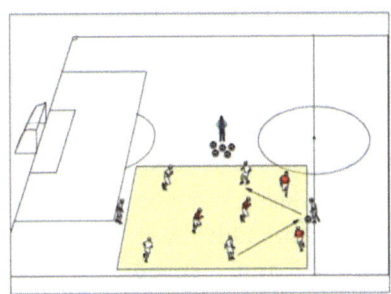

Figure 44. Auxiliary game 4x4 + 2 neutral players on the circuit.

4'

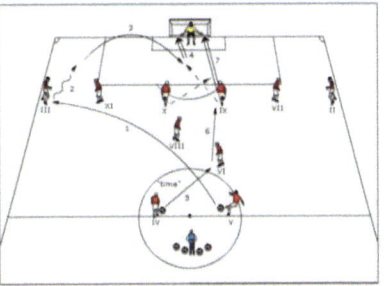

Figure 45. Scheme of playing the ball in a comprehensive exercise.

3'

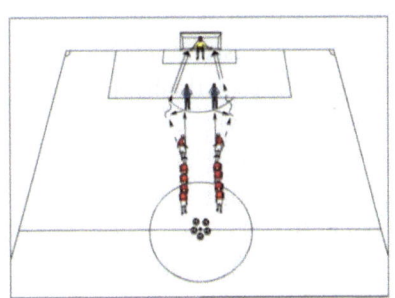

Figure 46. Shots on goal.

3.6. Pre-match warm-up of the team of the Polish Ekstraklasa - RKS Radomiak Radom

SELF OBSERVATION – DURATION [35']		
DRILLS	EXERCISE SETTING	TIME
I. **GENERAL PART** A) **Running and stretching exercises.** a) free individual run - any individual general development exercises,		10'

b) stretching exercises performed in a static way in a team setting with an emphasis on leg muscles (quadriceps, thighs' biceps and calf muscles),
c) team development exercises performed in a series (jogging, arm circles, leg kicks, jumping, skipping, abduction, adduction).

B) Coordination and speed exercises.
a) stretching exercises performed in a static way in a team setting with an emphasis on leg muscles (quadriceps, thighs' biceps and calf muscles) and general development exercises performed in place (torsion and twisting of the torso to the left, right, hip circles),
b) coordination and speed exercises, A-B-C skips in place for a quick start signal (forward, sideways and backward),
c) stretching exercises performed in a dynamic way in a team setting with an emphasis on leg muscles (quadriceps, thighs' biceps and calf muscles).

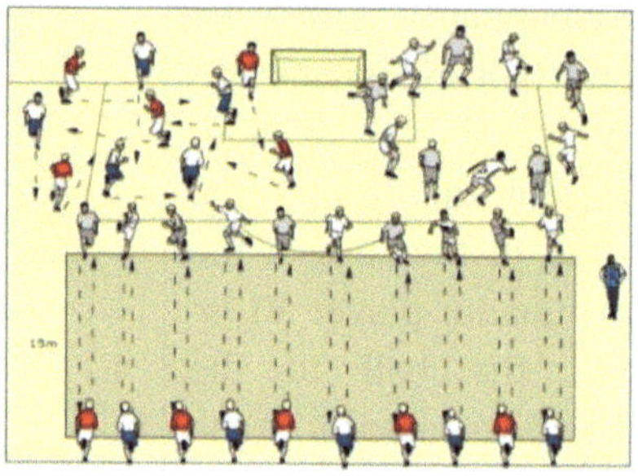

Figure 47. Exercises for running and stretching, general development without a ball and stretching exercises.

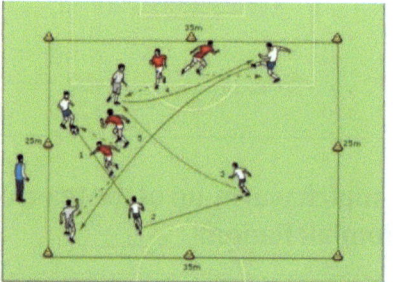

Figure 48. Coordination and speed exercises, static and dynamic stretching exercises.

8'

II. MAIN PART WITH BALLS
A) Numerical advantage for keeping the ball.
A 4x4 game plus 2 neutral players playing for possession of the ball on a pitch with dimensions of 35/25 meters. In this game, we care about keeping the ball playing smoothly. Two neutral players have the task of helping them keep possession of the ball for as long as possible. If the pressuring team has a problem recovering the ball, the players change at the signal of the coach. Those who are in possession of the ball are supposed to use

Figure 49. Numerical advantage 4x4 plus 2 neutral.

6'

their numerical advantage and maximize the field of play.

Number of touches - having the ball depending on the players' disposition on a given day max. 3 touches, preferably 1.

The first game - 2'30" (1" active rest - stretching).

Second game – 2'30".

B) **Exercises with balls – players matched in pairs (1 ball per pair).**
a) hitting the ball, with the inside part of the foot, thrown by the partner (10 times - LL and RL),
b) hitting the ball, with the laces, thrown by the partner (10 times - LL and RL),
c) heading the ball standing and jumping (8 times),
d) hitting the ball with the inside part of the foot on the ground on the first touch,
e) hitting the ball with the inside part of the foot on the ground with two touches (strong passes),
f) hitting the ball with the laces from a pass (in the air 30-40m away).

Figure 50. Exercises with the ball in pairs.

5'

III. **FINAL PART**
Exercises with a shot on goal.
a) side midfielder and defender on the right and left,
b) at the height of the penalty area centre defenders, midfielders, striker - 1, 8 cross pass, 2, 9 perpendicular pass, after dribbling the ball 5 and 12 cross the ball from the wing into the penalty area to the attackers (one player after a cross-over) definitely attacks the ball by hitting it on the ground.

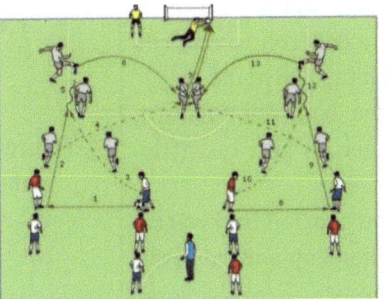

Figure 51. Exercise with a shot on goal.

6'

3.7. Goalkeeper pre-match warm-up proposal

OWN STUDY – DURATION [27']		
DRILLS	EXERCISE SETTING	TIME
I. GENERAL PART **Stretching exercises.** **Exercises in a trot:** a) arm circles forwards, backwards, forward sprints, reverse sprints, A-B-C skip, slides, side-steps to the right and left. **Exercises in place:** a) rotations, wrists, hips, torso, side stretch, torso twists, torso drop, b) sit straight, stretch to the right and left legs, from lying on the back, transition between supine and prone lying positions, from the position of the "bridge stretch", flipping forward, backward through standing on the shoulders, flipping through the right and left shoulder.	Figure 52. General development exercises without a ball – on the run, in a march and in place.	7'
II. MAIN PARTS WITH BALLS **Exercises with balls.** **Exercises within a field of sixteen meters.** a) throw the ball, roll forward, catch the ball in the air, b) throw the ball, roll backwards and catch the ball in the air, c) throw the ball, fall forward, quickly get up and catch the ball in the air, d) throw the ball, fall backwards, quickly stand up and catch the ball in the air, e) in the basic (goalkeeper) position, exercises with two balls, exchange the ball with the coach for 1-2-3, for three diving catches, returning the ball, get up quickly and practice further, trying to	Figure 53. Exercises with the ball – within a field of sixteen meters.	20'

maintain the continuity of the exercise. Repeat all of the exercises 6 times. **Goal exercises.** a) hitting the ball to the left and right of the goal, catching the ball in a fall, 4x on each side after the ball is caught by the goalkeeper within the central circle of the pitch, b) hitting the ball from a half-volley from 10m from the goal, catching the ball with a fall, 10 shots after the ball is caught, thrown by the goalkeeper to a marked place on the field.	 Figure 54. Hitting the ball in different sectors of the goal – by the coach.	

3.8. The goalkeeper warm-up performed before the match of F.C. Barcelona

BASED ON CICIRKO (Cicirko 2004) – DURATION [27']		
WORKS	**EXERCISE SETTING**	**TIME**
I. GENERAL PART **Exercises – stretching.** **Exercises from the post to the edge of the penalty box.** **A) Exercises in a trot:** a) shuffle - forwards, backwards, sideways, b) C skip (10x), c) A skip (10x), d) forward kicks (10x), e) loose running, f) arm circles backwards (10x), g) alternating wrist rotations, h) slow run. **Marching exercises.** a) back arches, b) as above with a torso twist, c) swing arms over head one at a time, alternating d) free walking. **B) Exercises in the goal area.** **Exercises in place:** a) stretching at the post, b) legs kicks forwards, backwards, to the sides,	Figure 55. General development exercises without a ball – on the run, in march and in place.	7'

c) kneeling stretching exercises (for both legs).

II. MAIN PART WITH BALLS.
Exercises with balls with a trainer.

a) light volleys from straight ahead of the goalkeeper, distance about 10-12 m (8-10x),
b) kicking the ball in the air once to a jump, once to the goalkeeper, distance about 10-12m (8-10x),
c) blocking a half-volley halfway up once to the right, once to the left, distance about 10-12m (10-12x),
d) blocking a ball from a half-volley downwards once to the right, once to the left, distance about 20m (10-12x),
e) an internal and laces (bottom and half-up) from the perimeter of the penalty area,
f) cross into the penalty area at the side of the pitch (the reserve goalkeeper is passively interrupting - 15x),
g) goalkeeper kicking the ball to the partners on both sides of the pitch (6x),
h) cross the ball (as above when crossing the ball) from the other side of the field,
i) cross on the left, from the centre and to the right of the pitch, from the goalkeeper's hand or on the ground (3x each),
j) hitting the ball with maximum strength in different sectors of the goal (down, half-way, top - 10x)
k) descent to the cloakroom.

20'

Figure 56. Exercises with the ball – passes by the trainer.

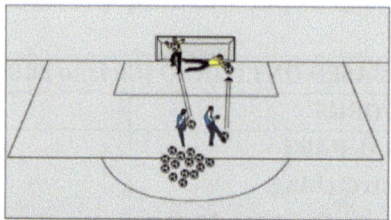

Figure 57. Hitting the ball in different sectors of the goal – by the coach.

As you can see, every coach of a team at a higher level prepares the body in a similar way. There are of course slight differences, because each leader has different participants. This is due to the diversity of personality in the team, as well as the level of training, or musculature of the player. I hope that the presented factors and examples of practical solutions affecting the preparation of the player's body will help in a better warm-up of the players for the competition. The presented tips can be used at all stages of development and it will be an important help for trainers and physical education teachers running teams in clubs or schools. In order to familiarize yourself with the pre-competition warm-ups in the Polish football premier league of the following teams: Wisła Kraków, Polonia Bytom, Korona Kielce and Odra Wodzisław, I recommend reading Talaga (2008, 2009) "Developmental content of the player's warm-up".

4. SUGGESTIONS FOR VARIOUS WARM-UP RUNS BEFORE TRAINING AND SCHOOL CLASSES

4.1. Universal warm-up course before training sessions

UNIVERSAL WARM-UP FOR TRAINING SESSIONS			
NO.	EXERCISE TYPE	WARM-UP	TIME
1.	**Slow running:** arms and legs exercises performed while running.	General	3-4 minutes
2.	**Torso exercises:** rotation of individual joints, rotating toe touches, etc.	General	2 minutes
3.	**Various stretching exercises:** performed dynamically or statically.	General	2 minutes
4.	**Exercises performed at an increased pace:** fast running, strengthening particularly heavily loaded muscles, multi-jumps combined with coordination exercises.	General	4-5 minutes
5.	**Various stretching exercises:** performed dynamically or statically.	General	2 minutes
6.	**Characteristic exercises for football:** dynamic coordination exercises developing optimal cooperation between muscles and nerves, special preparation for situations occurring in the game.	Special	12-15 minutes
	DURATION		25-30 minutes

4.1.1. Proposition of a general warm-up course without gear

PROPOSITION OF A WARM-UP BEFORE TRAINING			
General warm-up without accessories			
NO.	EXERCISE TYPE	ACCESSORIES	TIME
1.	**Slow running:** arms and legs exercises performed while running.	Without	3-4 minutes
2.	**Comprehensive trunk exercises** in four planes: forward and backward leans, hip circles, side twists, performed in-place.	Without	2 minutes
3.	**Various stretching exercises:** performed in a dynamic or static way, or by means of stretching.	Without	2 minutes
4.	**Exercises performed at an increased pace:** fast running, strengthening especially heavily loaded muscles, multi-jumps.	Without	4-5 minutes
5.	**Various stretching exercises:** performed in a dynamic or static way, or by means of stretching.	Without	2 minutes
6.	**Characteristic exercises for football:** dynamic coordination exercises performed with a partner to develop optimal cooperation between muscles and nerves.	Without	12-15 minutes
	DURATION		25-30 minutes

PROPOSITION OF A WARM-UP BEFORE SCHOOL CLASSES				
General warm-up without accessories				
NO.	EXERCISE TYPE	ACCESSORIES	TIME	
1.	Exercises performed in a slow run - arms and legs exercises.	Without	3 minutes	
2.	Stationary exercises - trunk exercises, rotation of individual joints, twists, etc.	Without	2 minutes	
3.	Dynamic exercises performed on the run - fast running, multi-jumps combined with coordination exercises.	Without	3 minutes	
4.	Stretching exercises performed dynamically.	Without	2 minutes	
5.	Coordination exercises performed with a partner.	Without	2 minutes	
DURATION				12 minutes

4.1.2. Proposition of a general warm-up course with gear other than a ball

PROPOSITION OF A WARM-UP BEFORE TRAINING				
A general warm-up with equipment other than a ball				
NO.	EXERCISE TYPE	ACCESSORIES	TIME	
1.	**Slow running** - arms and legs exercises performed while running	Any	3-4 minutes	
2.	**Comprehensive torso exercises** - in four planes: forward and backward leans, hip circles, side twists, performed in-place.	Any	2 minutes	
3.	**Various stretching exercises:** performed in a dynamic or static way, or by means of stretching.	Any	2 minutes	
4.	**Exercises performed at an increased pace:** fast running, strengthening especially heavily loaded muscles, multi-jumps.	Any	4-5 minutes	
5.	**Various stretching exercises** - performed in a dynamic or static way, or by means of stretching.	Any	2 minutes	
6.	**Characteristic football exercises** - dynamic coordination exercises with equipment e.g. coordination ladder, coordination platform, etc., developing optimal cooperation between muscles and nerves.	Any	12-15 minutes	
DURATION				25-30 minutes

PROPOSITION OF A WARM-UP BEFORE SCHOOL CLASSES			
A general warm-up with equipment other than the ball			
NO.	EXERCISE TYPE	ACCESSORIES	TIME
1.	Exercises performed in a slow run - arms and legs exercises.	Any	2 minutes
2.	Stationary exercises - trunk exercises, rotation of individual joints, rotating toe touches, etc.	Any	2 minutes
3.	Dynamic exercises performed on the run - fast running, multi-jumps combined with coordination exercises.	Any	2 minutes
4.	Flexibility exercises performed dynamically.	Any	2 minutes
5.	Coordination exercises with accessories e.g. coordination ladder, coordination platform, etc.	Any	4 minutes
	DURATION		12 minutes

4.1.3. Proposition of a warm-up with a ball

PROPOSITION OF A WARM-UP BEFORE TRAINING			
Development warm-up with a ball			
NO.	EXERCISE TYPE	ACCESSORIES	TIME
1.	**Slow running** - arms and legs exercises performed in a slow run.	Ball	3-4 minutes
2.	**Comprehensive torso exercises** - in four planes: forward and backward leans, hip circles, side twists, performed in-place.	Ball	2 minutes
3.	**Various stretching exercises:** performed in a dynamic or static way, or by means of stretching.	Ball	2 minutes
4.	**Exercises performed at an increased pace:** fast running, strengthening especially heavily loaded muscles, multi-jumps.	Ball	4-5 minutes
5.	**Various stretching exercises** - performed in a dynamic or static way, or by means of stretching.	Ball	2 minutes
6.	**Characteristic football exercises** - dynamic coordination exercises with the ball that develop optimal cooperation between muscles and nerves.	Ball	12-15 minutes
	DURATION		25-30 minutes

PROPOSITION OF A WARM-UP BEFORE SCHOOL CLASSES			
Development warm-up with a ball			
NO.	EXERCISE TYPE	ACCESSORIES	TIME
1.	Exercises performed in a slow run - arms and legs exercises.	Ball	2 minutes
2.	Stationary exercises - trunk exercises, rotation of individual joints, twists, etc.	Ball	2 minutes

3.	Dynamic exercises performed on the run - fast running, multi-jumps combined with coordination exercises.	Ball	2 minutes
4.	Stretching exercises performed dynamically.	Ball	2 minutes
5.	Coordination exercises with the ball.	Ball	4 minutes
	DURATION		12 minutes

4.1.4. Proposition of a warm-up course with a ball and special technique elements

PROPOSITION OF A WARM-UP BEFORE TRAINING			
A warm-up with a ball and special technique elements			
NO.	EXERCISE TYPE	ACCESSORIES	TIME
1.	**Slow running** - arms and legs exercises performed in a slow run.	Ball	3-4 minutes
2.	**Comprehensive trunk exercises** - in four planes: forward and backward leans, hip circles, side twists, performed in-place.	Ball	2 minutes
3.	**Various stretching exercises:** performed in a dynamic or static way, or by means of stretching.	Ball	2 minutes
4.	**Exercises performed at an increased pace:** fast running, strengthening especially heavily loaded muscles, multi-jumps.	Ball	4-5 minutes
5.	**Various stretching exercises** - performed in a dynamic or static way, or by means of stretching.	Ball	2 minutes
6.	**Characteristic football exercises** - special preparation for game situations (special technique exercises performed in motion).	Ball	12-15 minutes
	DURATION		25-30 minutes

PROPOSITION OF A WARM-UP BEFORE SCHOOL CLASSES			
A warm-up with a ball and special technique elements			
NO.	EXERCISE TYPE	ACCESSORIES	TIME
1.	Exercises performed in a slow run - arms and legs exercises.	Ball	2 minutes
2.	Stationary exercises - trunk exercises, rotation of individual joints, twisted turns, etc.	Ball	2 minutes
3.	Dynamic exercises performed on the run - fast running, multi-jumps combined with coordination exercises.	Ball	2 minutes
4.	Stretching exercises performed dynamically.	Ball	2 minutes
5.	Special technique exercises performed in motion.	Ball	4 minutes
	DURATION		12 minutes

4.1.5. Proposition of a warm-up course with a ball and tactical elements

PROPOSITION OF A WARM-UP BEFORE TRAINING			
A warm-up with a ball and elements of tactics			
NO.	EXERCISE TYPE	ACCESSORIES	TIME
1.	**Slow running** - arms and legs exercises performed in a slow run.	Ball	3-4 minutes
2.	**Comprehensive trunk exercises -** in four planes: forward and backward leans, hip circles, side twists, performed in-place.	Ball	2 minutes
3.	**Various stretching exercises:** performed in a dynamic or static way, or by means of stretching.	Ball	2 minutes
4.	**Exercises performed at an increased pace:** fast running, strengthening especially heavily loaded muscles, multi-jumps.	Ball	4-5 minutes
5.	**Various stretching exercises** - performed in a dynamic or static way, or by means of stretching.	Ball	2 minutes
6.	**Characteristic football exercises -** special preparation for game situations (special technique exercises performed in motion, including elements of game tactics).	Ball	12-15 minutes
	DURATION		25-30 minutes

PROPOSITION OF A WARM-UP BEFORE SCHOOL CLASSES			
A warm-up with a ball and elements of tactics			
NO.	EXERCISE TYPE	ACCESSORIES	TIME
1.	Exercises performed in a slow run - arms and legs exercises.	Ball	2 minutes
2.	Stationary exercises - trunk exercises, rotation of individual joints, twisted turns, etc.	Ball	1 minute
3.	Dynamic exercises performed on the run - fast running, multi-jumps combined with coordination exercises.	Ball	2 minutes
4.	Stretching exercises performed dynamically.	Ball	2 minutes
5.	Special technique exercises performed in motion, including elements of game tactics.	Ball	5 minutes
	DURATION		12 minutes

4.1.6. Proposition of a combined warm-up (mixed) course

PROPOSITION OF A WARM-UP BEFORE TRAINING			
Combined warm-up (mixed)			
NO.	EXERCISE TYPE	ACCESSORIES	TIME
1.	**Slow running** - arms and legs exercises performed in a slow run.	Any or none	3-4 minutes
2.	**Comprehensive trunk exercises** - in four planes: forward and backward leans, hip circles, side twists, performed in place.	Any or none	2 minutes
3.	**Various stretching exercises:** performed in a dynamic or static way, or by means of stretching.	Any or none	2 minutes
4.	**Exercises performed at an increased pace:** fast running, strengthening especially heavily loaded muscles, multi-jumps.	Any or none	4-5 minutes
5.	**Various stretching exercises** - performed in a dynamic or static way, or by means of stretching.	Any or none	2 minutes
6.	**Characteristic exercises for football** - dynamic coordination exercises with equipment e.g. coordination ladder, coordination platform, etc., developing optimal cooperation between muscles and nerves, special preparation for situations occurring in the game (special technique exercises performed with ball movement).	Ball and other gear	10 minutes
	DURATION		25 minutes

PROPOSITION OF A WARM-UP BEFORE SCHOOL CLASSES			
Combined warm-up (mixed)			
NO.	EXERCISE TYPE	ACCESSORIES	TIME
1.	Exercises performed in a slow run - arms and legs exercises.	Any or none	2 minutes
2.	Stationary exercises - trunk exercises, rotations of individual joints, twisted turns, etc.	Any or none	1 minute
3.	Dynamic exercises performed on the run - fast running, multi-jumps combined with coordination exercises.	Any or none	2 minutes
4.	Stretching exercises performed dynamically.	Any or none	2 minutes
5.	Special technique exercises performed with a ball, movement and coordination exercises with accessories, e.g. coordination ladder, coordination platform, etc.	Ball and other gear	5 minutes
	DURATION		12 minutes

4.1.7. Proposition of a goalkeeper warm-up course

PROPOSITION OF A WARM-UP BEFORE TRAINING			
Goalkeeper warm up			
NO.	EXERCISE TYPE	ACCESSORIES	TIME
1.	**Slow running -** arms and legs exercises performed in a slow run.	Any or none	3-4 minutes
2.	**Comprehensive trunk exercises -** in four planes: forward and backward leans, hip circles, side twists, performed in-place.	Any or none	2 minutes
3.	**Various stretching exercises:** performed in a dynamic or static way, or by means of stretching.	Any or none	2 minutes
4.	**Exercises -** performed without a ball.	Any or none	4-5 minutes
5.	**Various stretching exercises -** performed in a dynamic or static way, or by means of stretching.	Any or none	2 minutes
6.	**Exercises -** performed with the ball.	Ball and other gear	12-15 minutes
	DURATION		25-30 minutes

PROPOSITION OF A WARM-UP BEFORE SCHOOL CLASSES			
Goalkeeper warm-up			
NO.	EXERCISE TYPE	ACCESSORIES	TIME
1.	Exercises performed in a slow run - arms and legs exercises.	Any or none	2 minutes
2.	Stationary exercises - trunk exercises, rotations of individual joints, twists, etc.	Any or none	1 minute
3.	Stretching exercises performed in a dynamic and static way.	Any or none	2 minutes
4.	Exercises performed without a ball.	Any or none	2 minutes
5.	Exercises performed with a ball.	Ball and other gear	5 minutes
	DURATION		12 minutes

5. SUGGESTIONS FOR TRAINING SETTINGS USED TO WARM-UP

5.1. Suggestions of training settings that can be used in general development warm-up without accessories

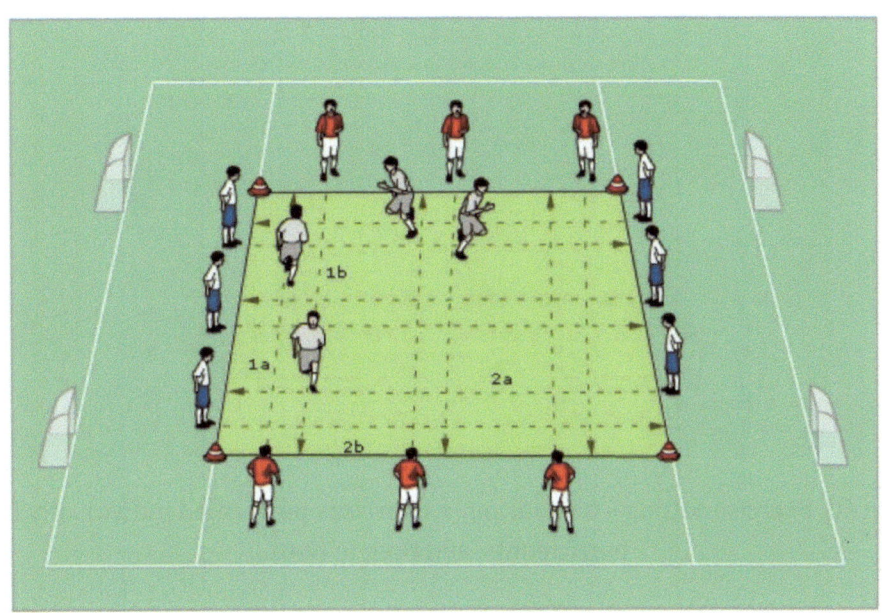

Figure 58. Exercise setting - a quadrangle, exercises performed individually by the participants.

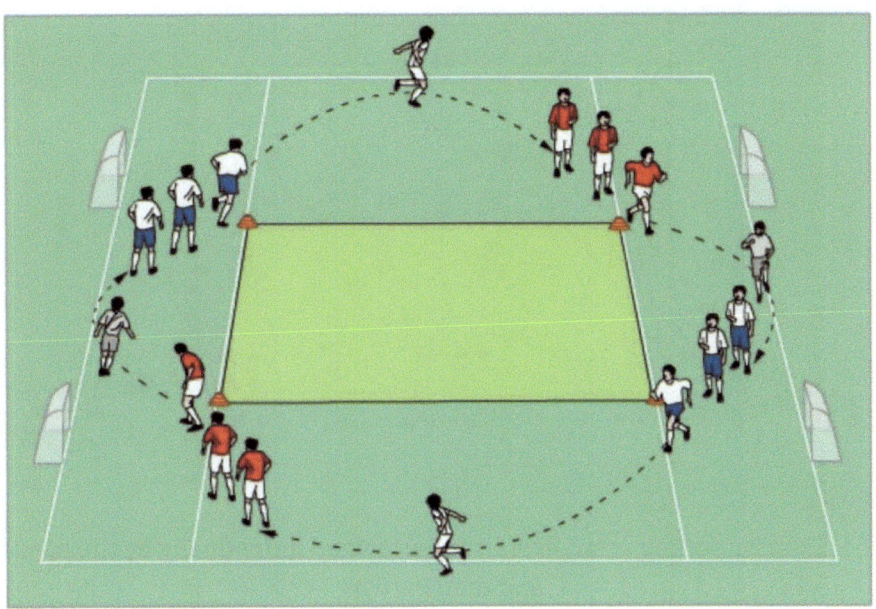

Figure 59. Exercise setting - a quadrangle, exercises performed individually by the participants.

Figure 60. Exercise setting – a quadrangle, exercises performed individually by the participants, and then in twos.

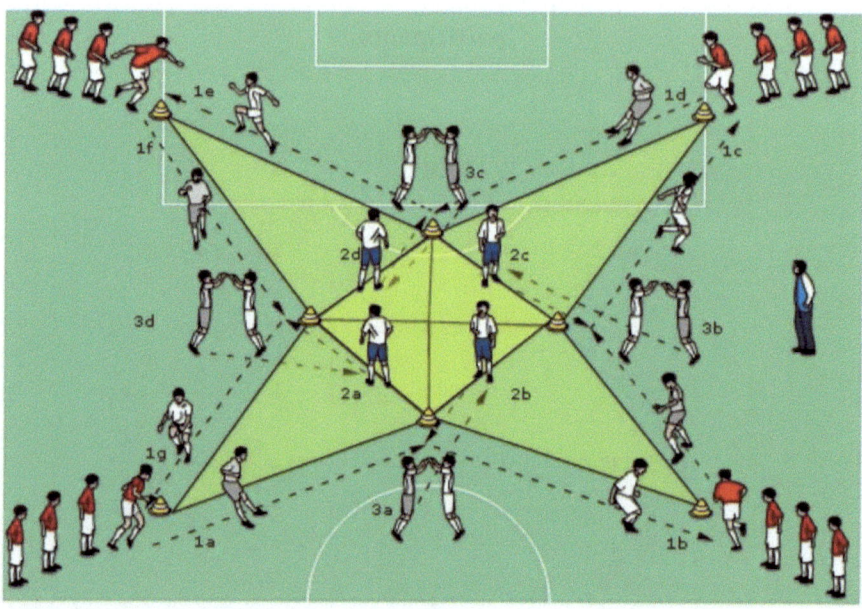

Figure 61. Exercise setting - star, exercises performed individually by the participants, and then in twos.

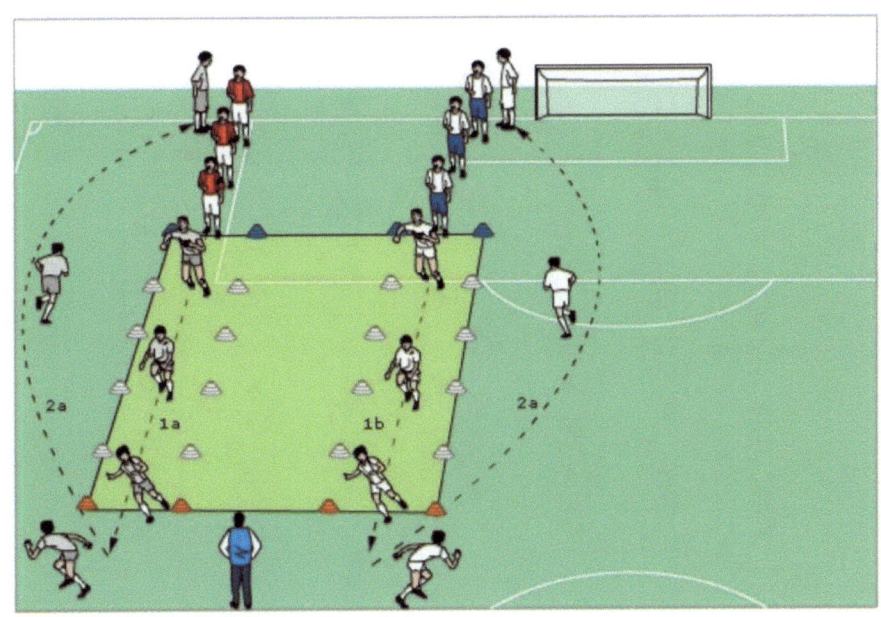

Figure 62. Exercise setting - queues, exercises performed individually by the participants.

Figure 63. Exercise setting - queues, exercises performed individually by the participants.

Figure 64. Exercise setting - queues, exercises performed collectively by the participants, and then in twos.

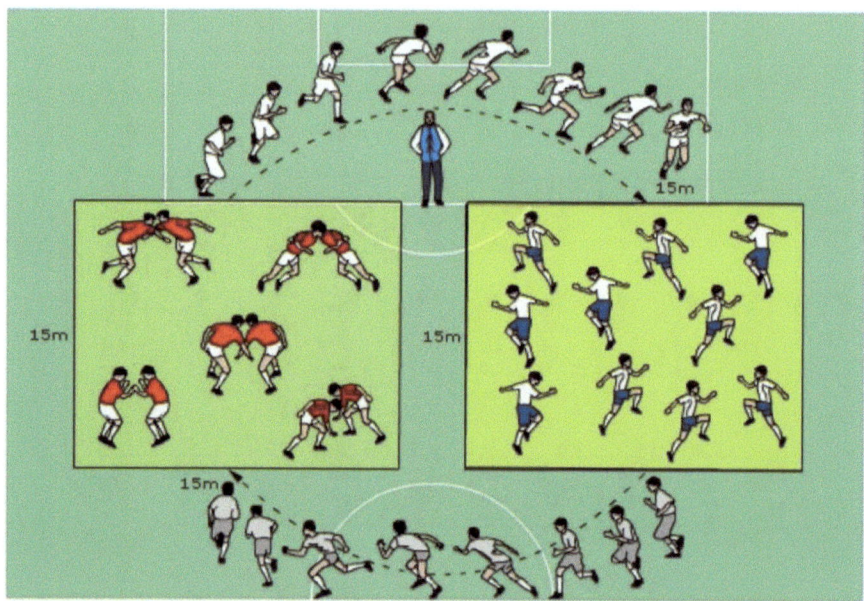

Figure 65. Exercise setting – a loose cluster, exercises performed individually by half of the exercisers, and the other half performs exercises in twos.

Figure 66. Exercise setting - a loose cluster, exercises performed individually, exercises are performed in pairs on signal.

Figure 67. Exercise setting - a loose cluster, exercises performed in twos.

Figure 68. Exercise setting - circle, exercises performed individually by the participants.

5.2. Suggestions of training settings that can be used in a general development warm-up using equipment other than a ball

Figure 69. Exercise setting - a loose cluster, exercises performed individually by the participants.

Figure 70. Exercise setting - a loose cluster, exercises performed individually by the participants.

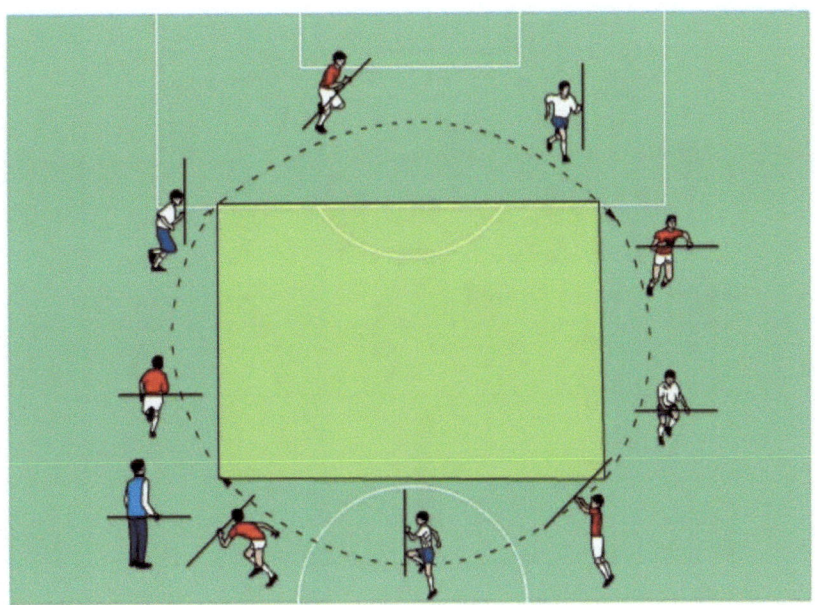

Figure 71. Exercise setting - circle, exercises performed individually by the participants.

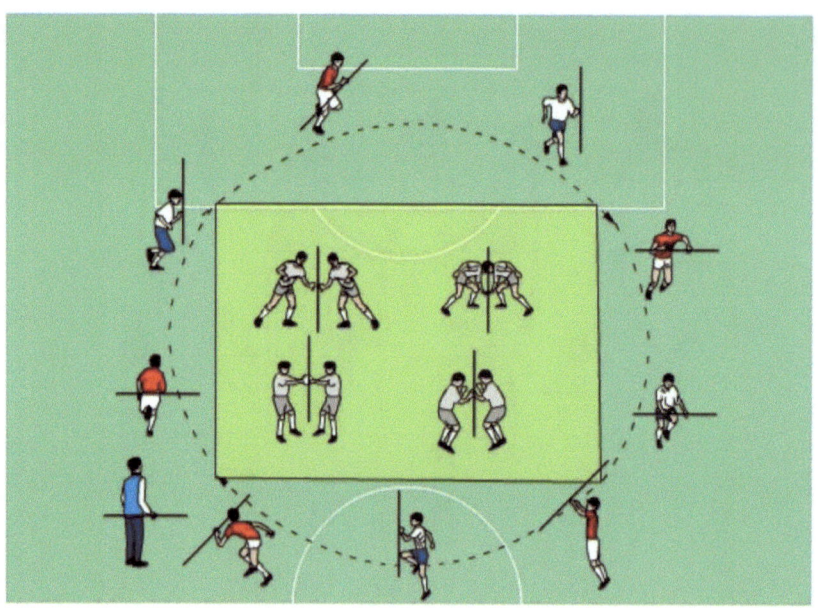

Figure 72. Exercise setting – circle, exercises performed individually by half of the exercisers, and the other half performs exercises in twos.

Figure 73. Exercise setting - a loose cluster, exercises performed individually by the participants.

Figure 74. Exercise setting - a loose cluster, exercises performed in twos.

Figure 75. Exercise setting - a loose cluster, exercises performed individually by the participants.

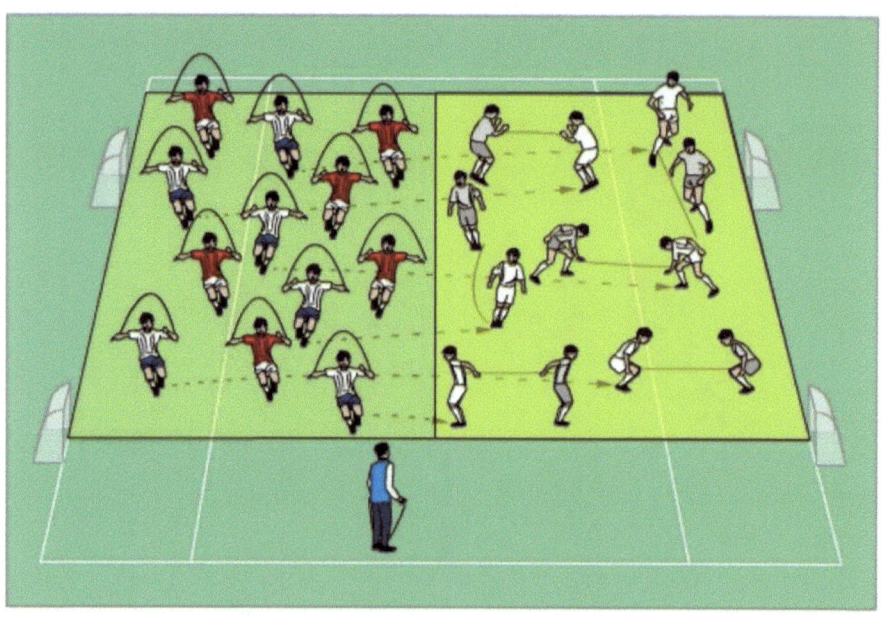

Figure 76. Exercise setting – a loose cluster, exercises performed individually by the participants, and then in twos.

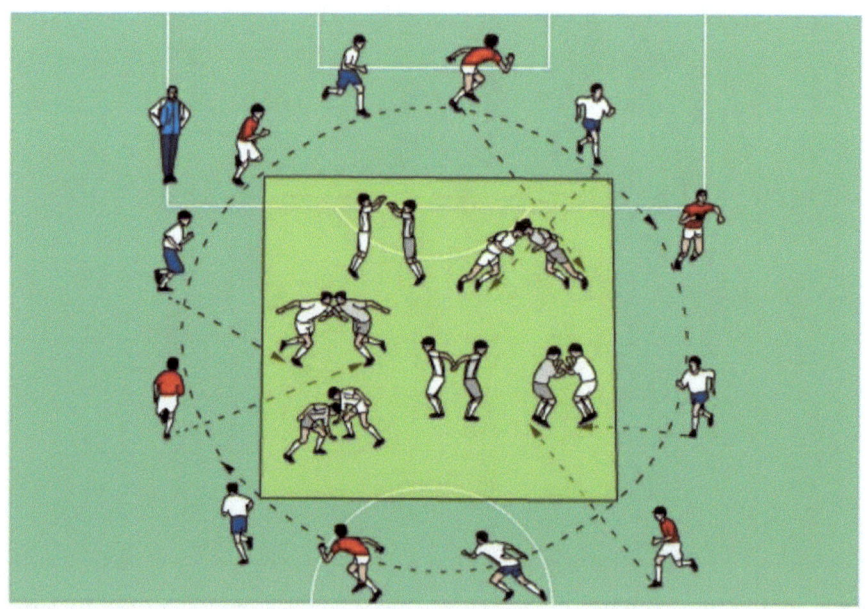

Figure 77. Exercise setting – circle, exercises performed individually by the participants, and then in twos.

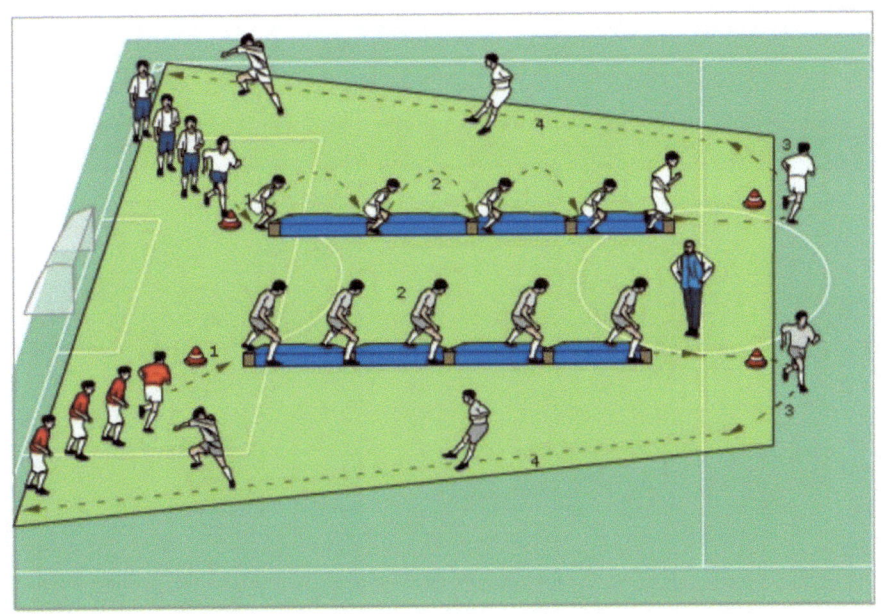

Figure 78. Exercise setting - queues, exercises performed individually by the participants.

Figure 79. Exercise setting - a loose bunch, exercises performed in twos.

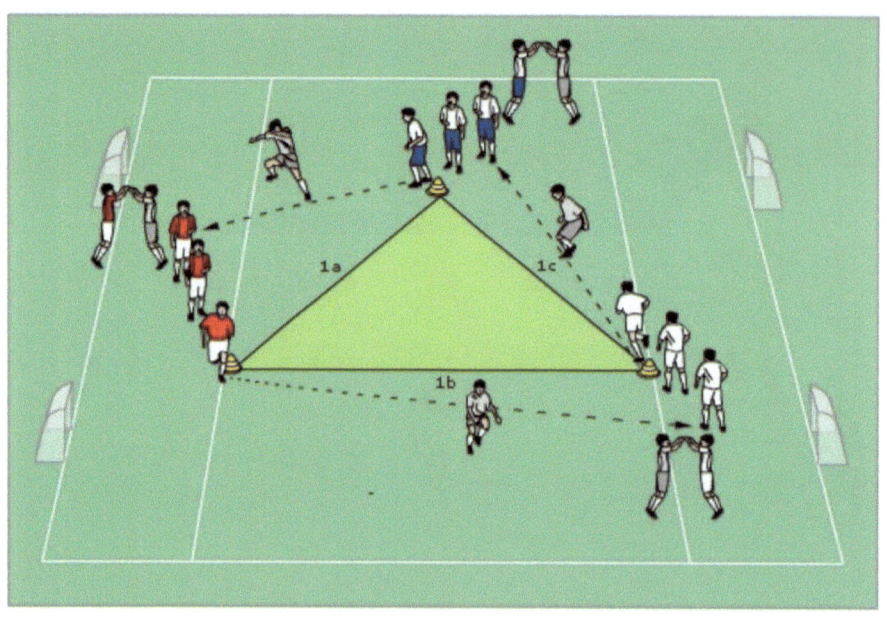

Figure 80. Exercise setting – triangle, exercises performed individually by the participants, and then in twos.

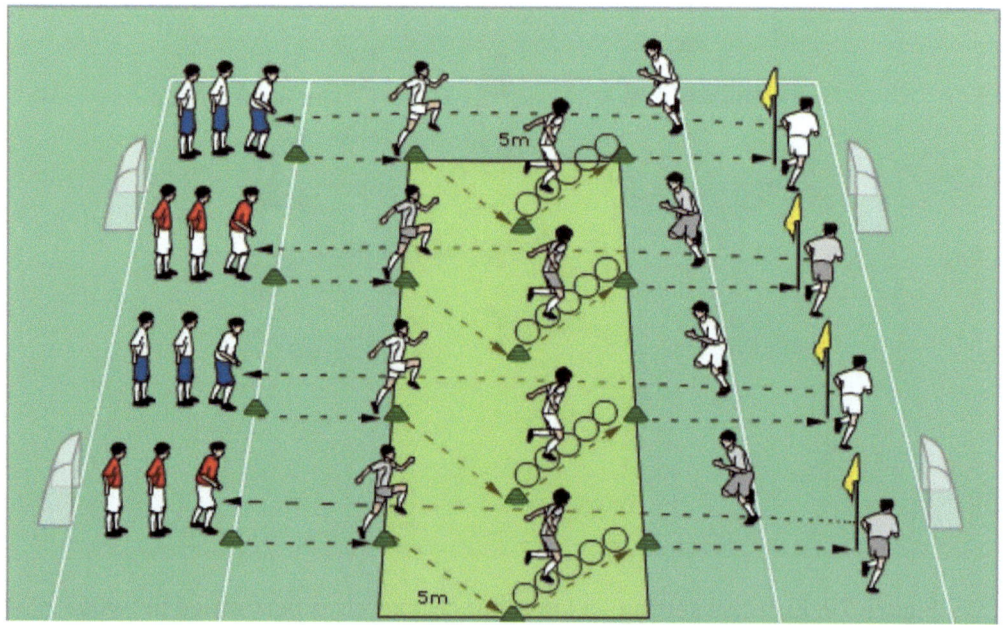

Figure 81. Exercise setting - queues, exercises performed individually by the participants.

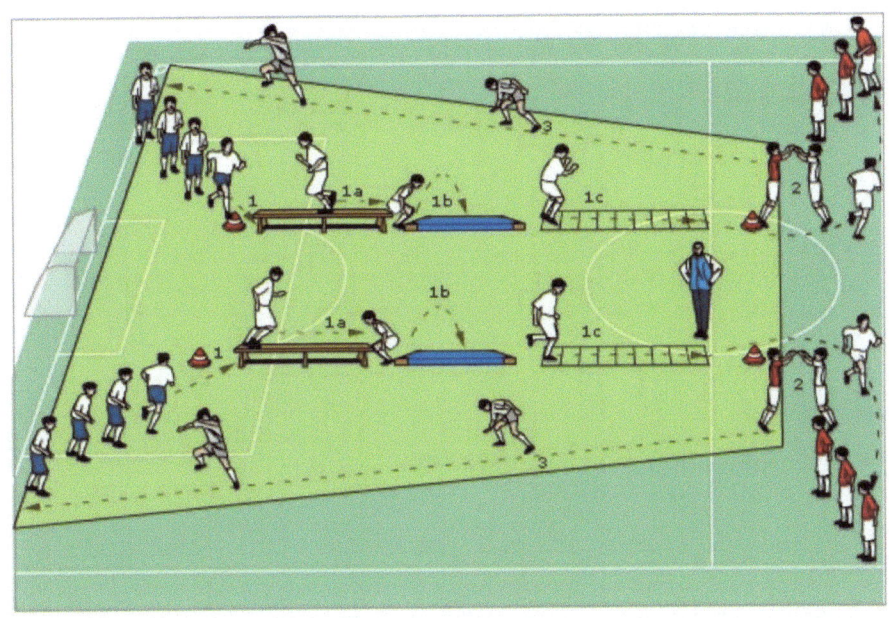

Figure 82. Exercise setting - queues, exercises performed individually by the participants, and then in twos.

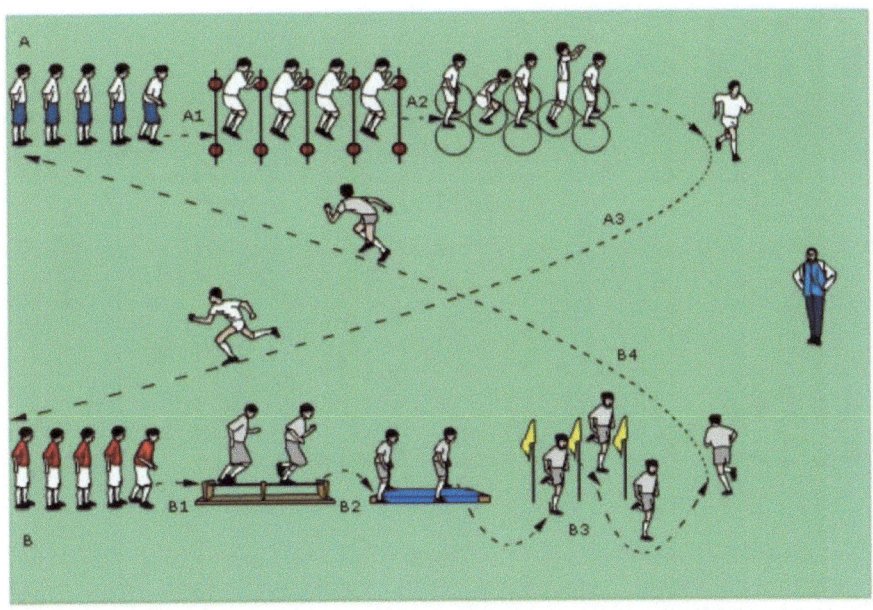

Figure 83. Exercise setting - queues, exercises performed individually by the participants.

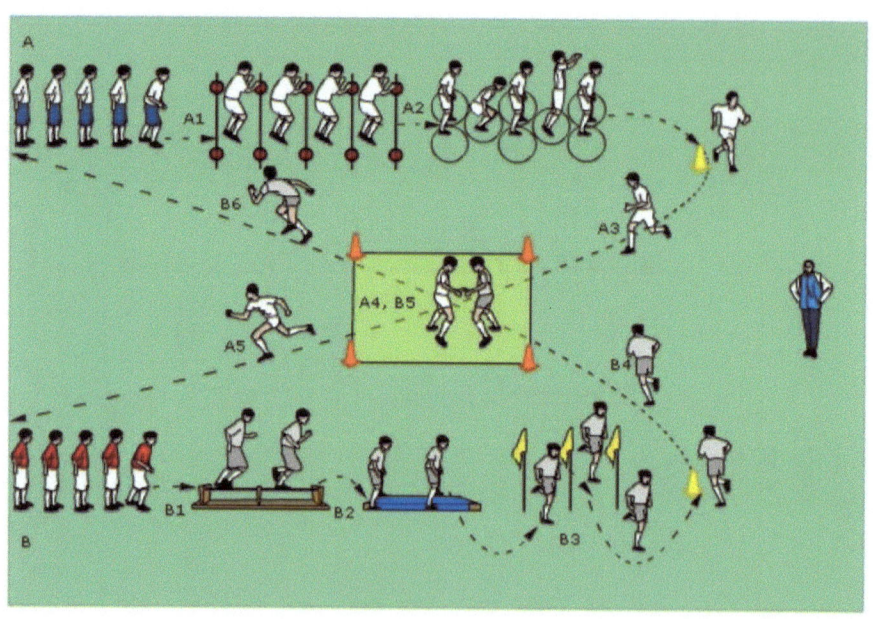

Figure 84. Exercise setting - queues, exercises performed individually by the participants, and then in twos.

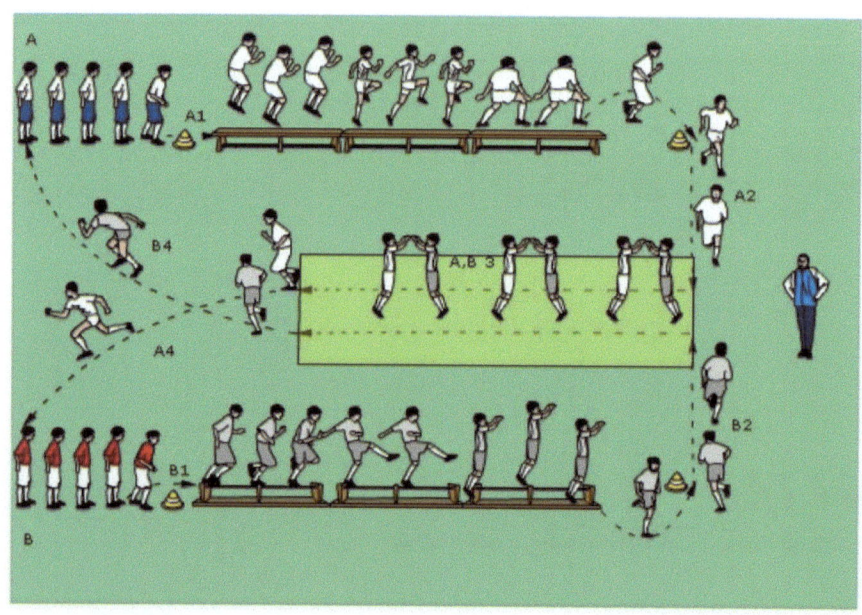

Figure 85. Exercise setting - queues, exercises performed individually by the participants, and then in twos.

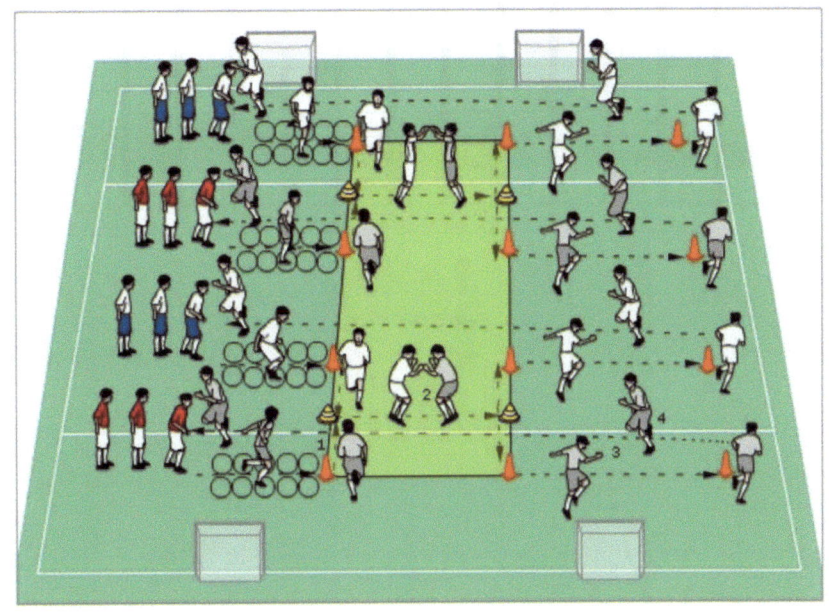

Figure 86. Exercise setting - queues, exercises performed individually by the participants, and then in twos.

Figure 87. Exercise setting – queues, exercises performed individually by the participants, and then in twos.

Figure 88. Exercise setting - queues, exercises performed individually by the participants.

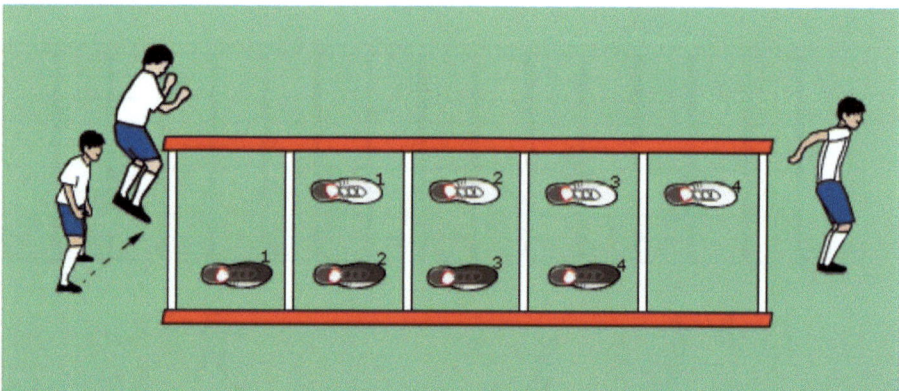
Figure 89. Exercise setting - queues, exercises performed individually by the participants.

5.3. Suggestions of training settings that can be used in a general warm-up with a ball

Figure 90. Exercise setting – a loose bunch, exercises performed individually by the participants.

Figure 91. Exercise setting - queues, exercises performed individually by the participants.

Figure 92. Exercise setting - queues, exercises performed individually by the participants.

Figure 93. Exercise setting - queues, exercises performed individually by the participants.

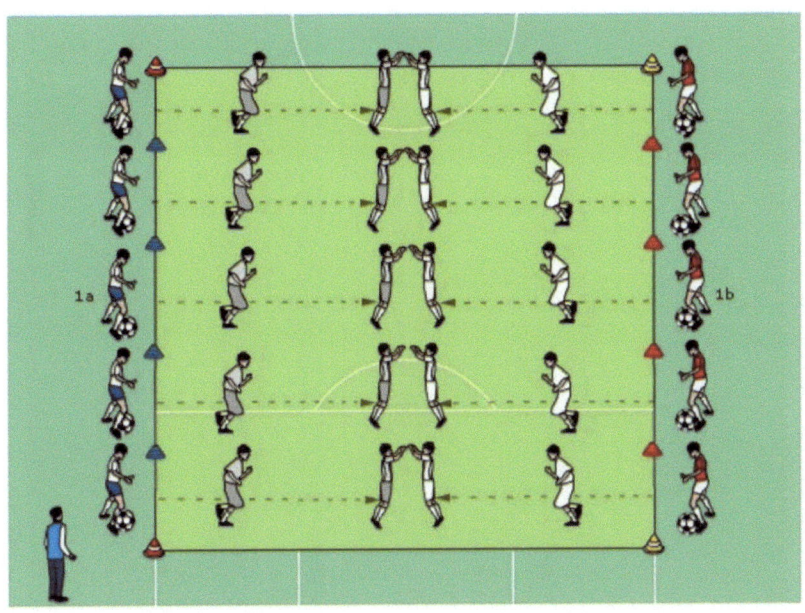

Figure 94. Exercise setting – queues, exercises performed individually by the participants, and then in twos.

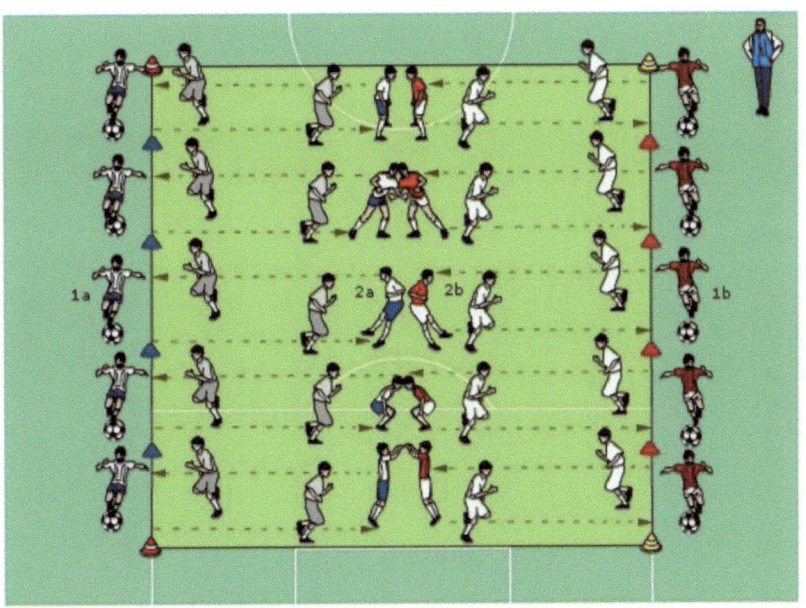

Figure 95. Exercise setting – queues, exercises performed individually by the participants, and then in twos.

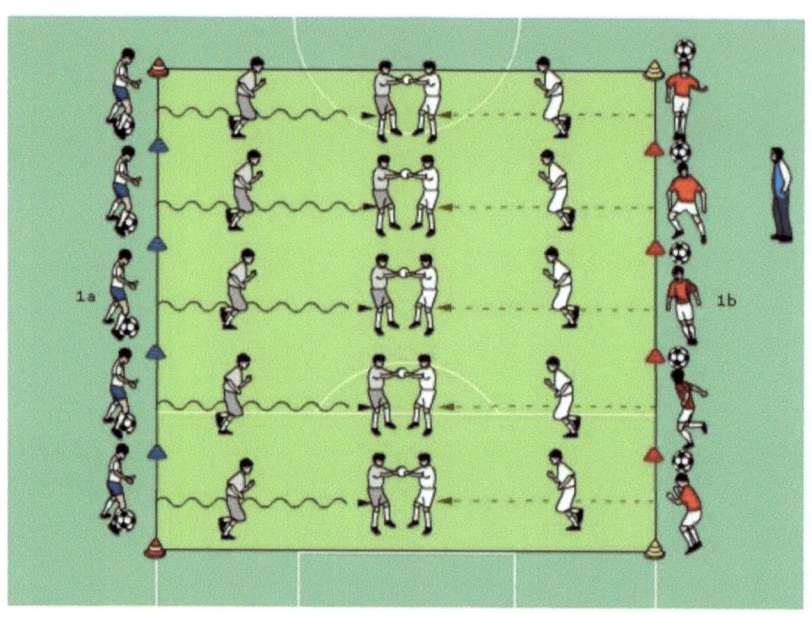

Figure 96. Exercise setting – queues, exercises performed individually by the participants, and then in twos.

Figure 97. Exercise setting - queues, exercises performed individually by the participants, and then in twos.

Figure 98. Exercise setting - a loose bunch, exercises performed in twos.

Figure 99. Exercise setting - a quadrangle, exercises performed individually by the participants.

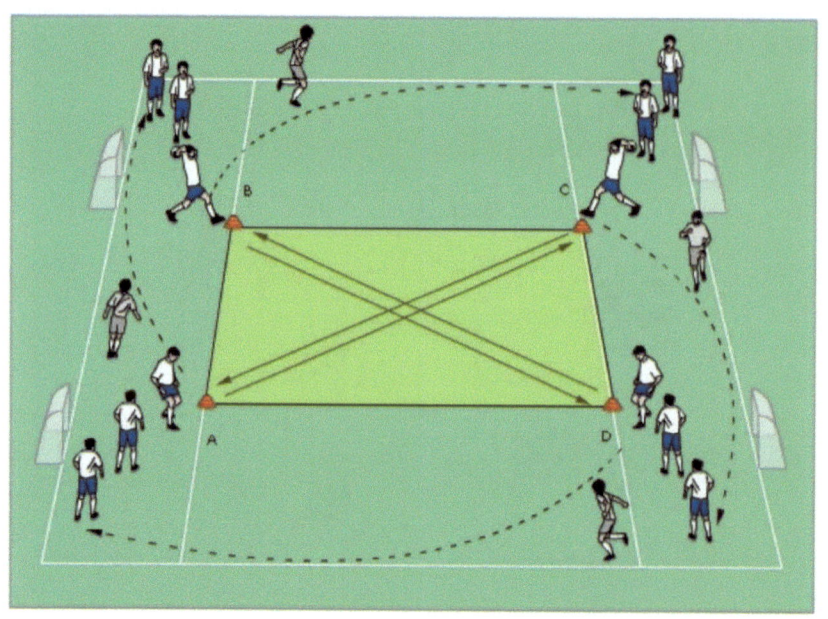

Figure 100. Exercise setting - a quadrangle, exercises performed individually by the participants.

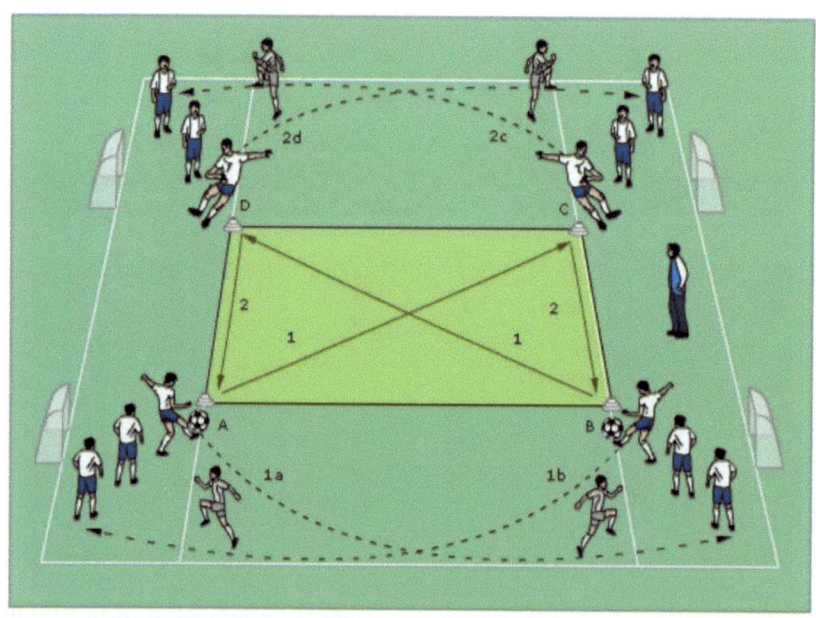

Figure 101. Exercise setting - a quadrangle, exercises performed individually by the participants.

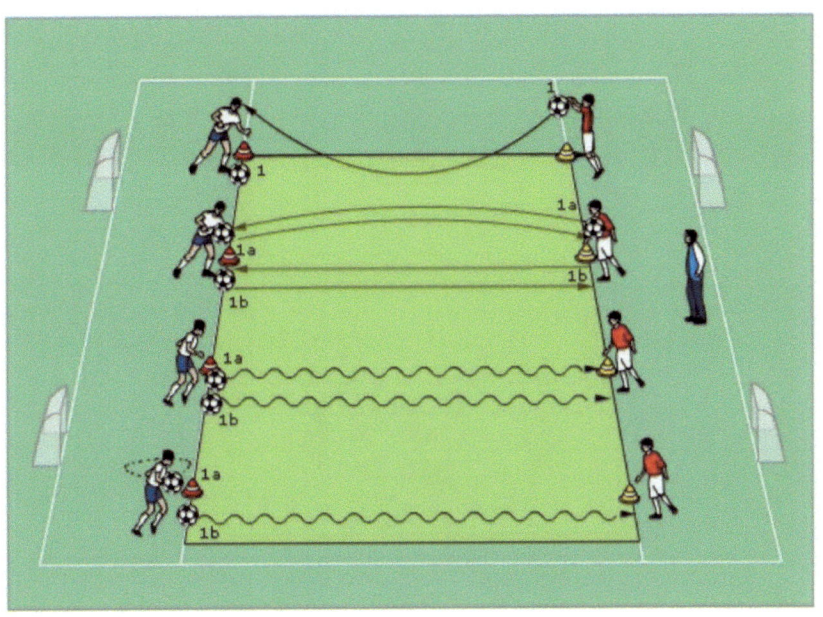

Figure 102. Exercise setting - a quadrangle, exercises performed in twos.

Figure 103. Exercise setting - a quadrangle, exercises performed individually by the participants.

79

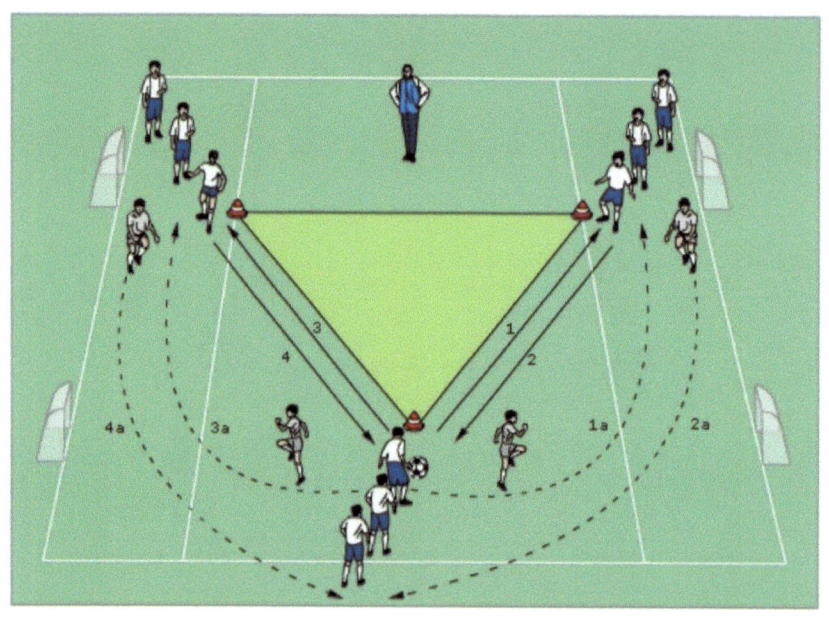

Figure 104. Exercise setting – triangle, exercises performed individually by the participants.

Figure 105. Exercise setting - queues, exercises performed in a group by half of the exercisers, and the other half performs exercises in twos.

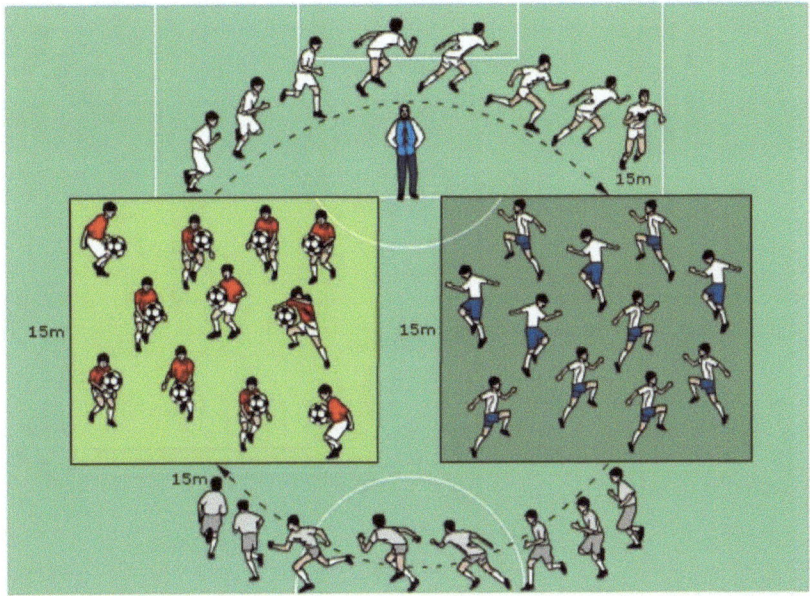

Figure 106. Exercise setting – a loose bunch, exercises performed individually by half of the players with a ball, and the other half performs exercises without a ball.

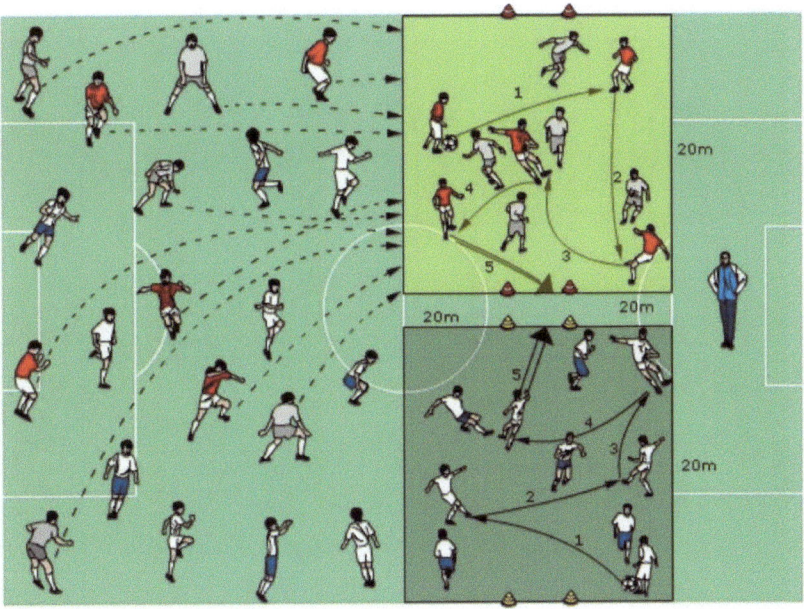

Figure 107. Exercise setting – a loose bunch, exercises performed individually by half of the players, and the other half performs in a group.

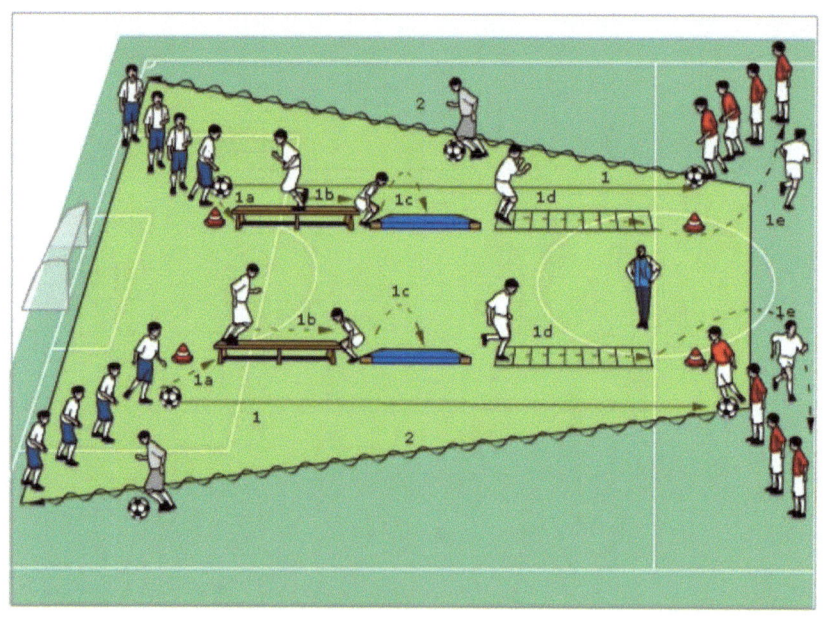

Figure 108. Exercise setting – queues, exercises performed individually by the participants.

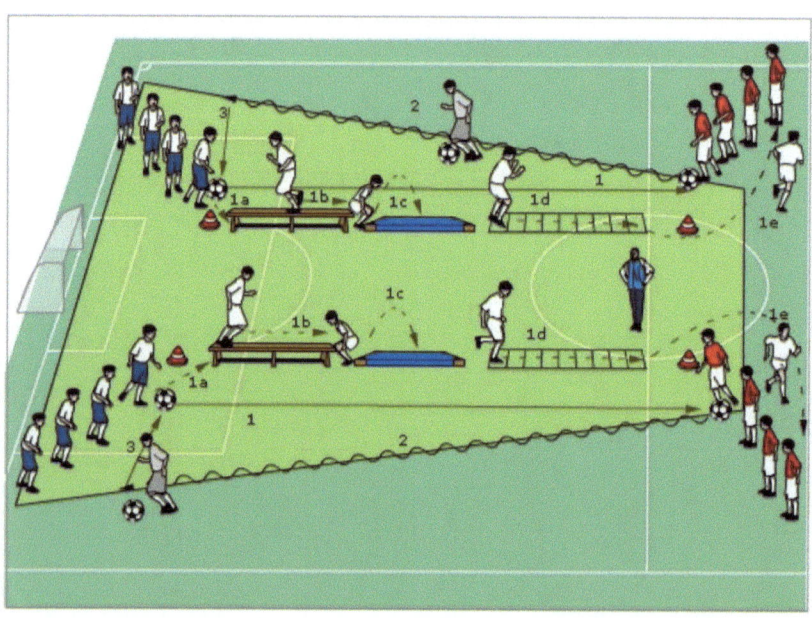

Figure 109. Exercise setting – queues, exercises performed individually by the participants.

5.4. Suggestions of training settings that can be used in a focused warm-up with a ball and special technique elements

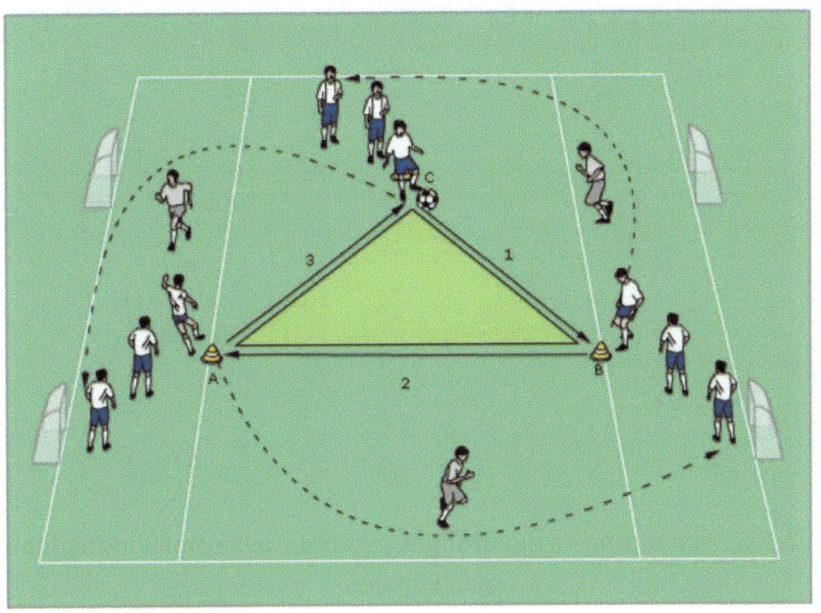

Figure 110. Exercise setting - triangle, exercises performed individually by the participants.

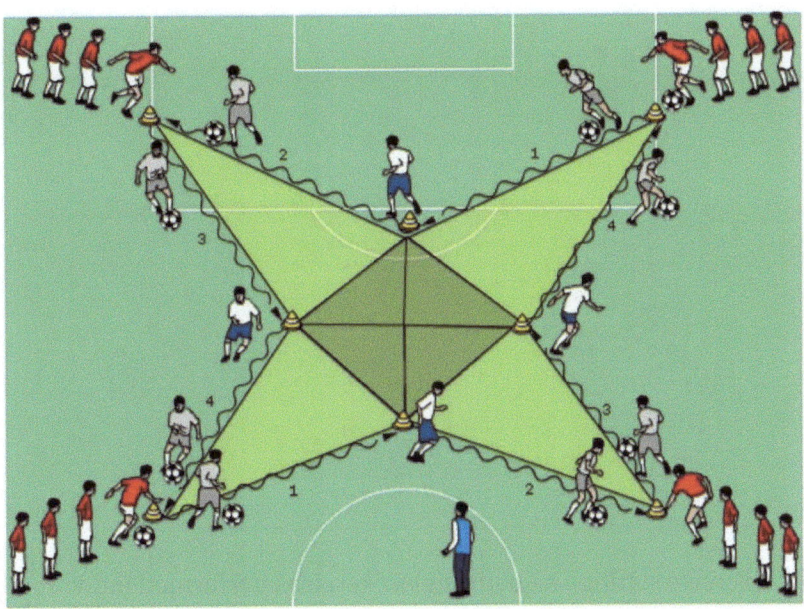

Figure 111. Exercise setting - star, exercises performed individually by the players.

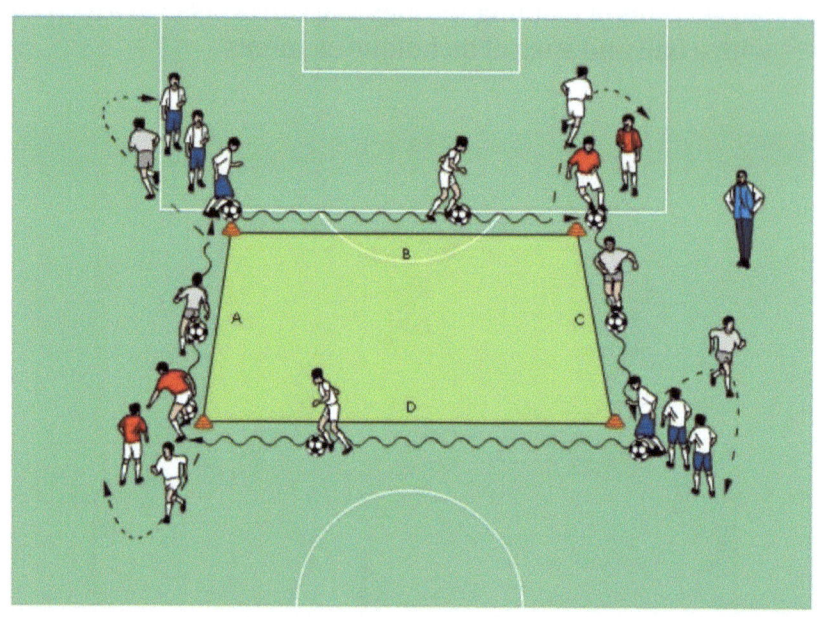

Figure 112. Exercise setting - a quadrangle, exercises performed individually by the participants.

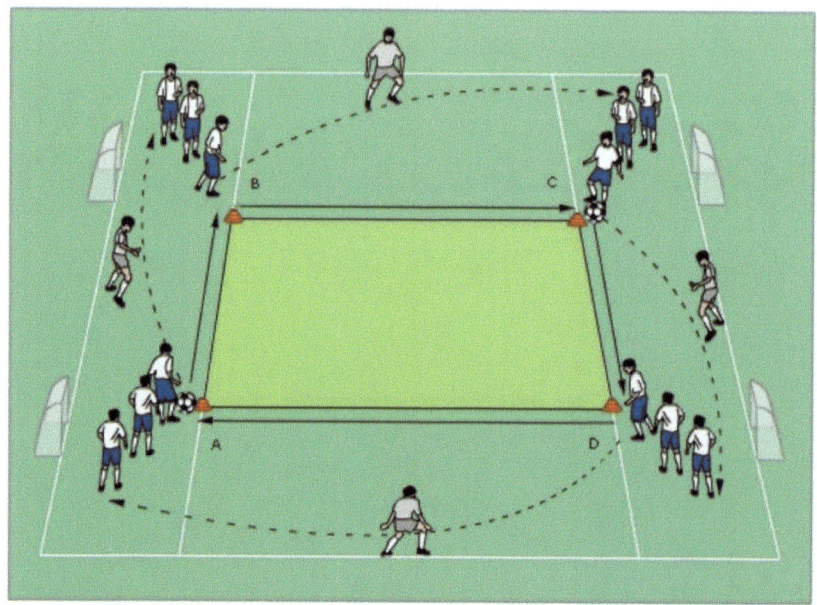

Figure 113. Exercise setting - a quadrangle, exercises performed individually by the participants.

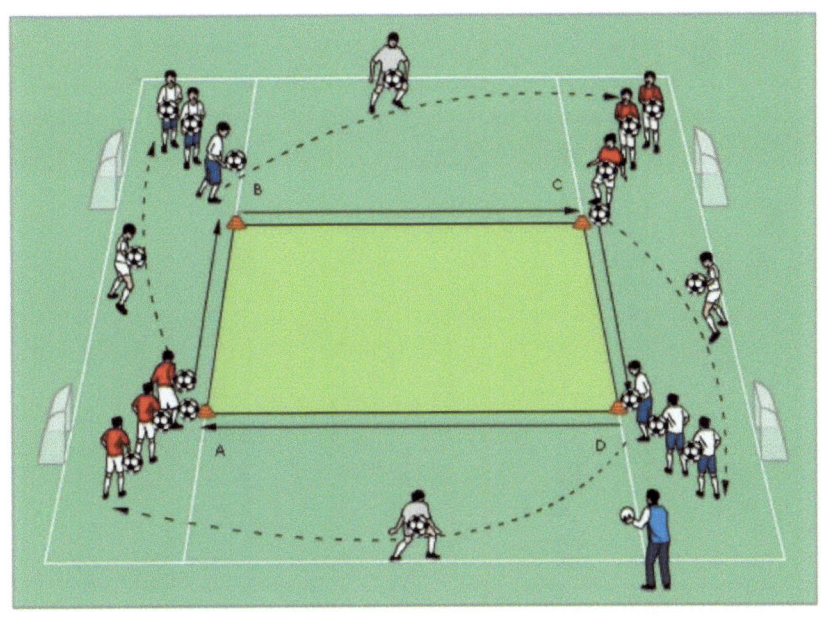

Figure 114. Exercise setting - a quadrangle, exercises performed individually by the participants.

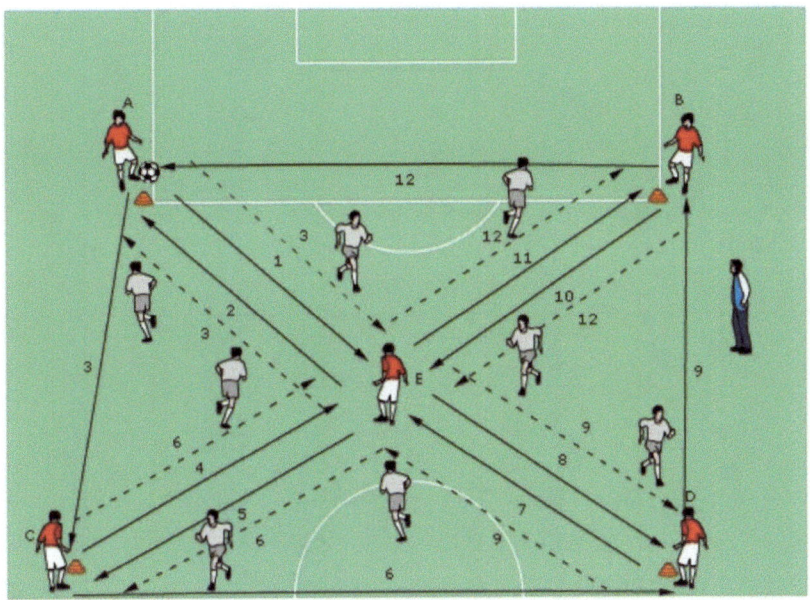

Figure 115. Exercise setting - a quadrangle, exercises performed individually by the participants.

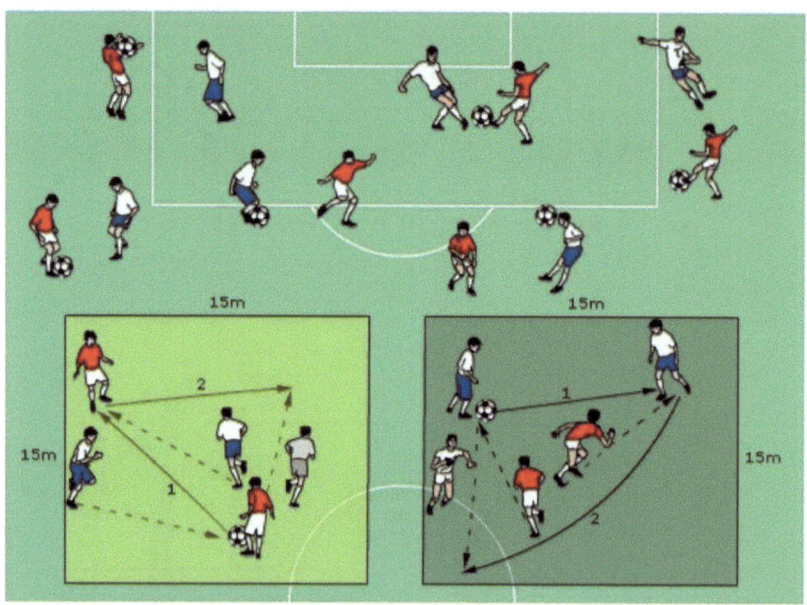

Figure 116. Exercise setting – a loose bunch, exercises performed in a group by half of the exercisers, and the other half performs exercises in twos.

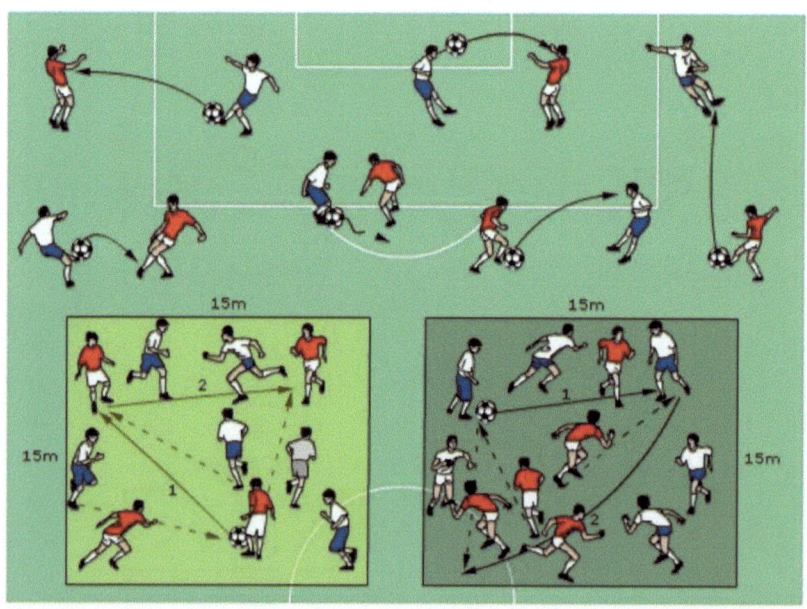

Figure 117. Exercise setting – a loose bunch, exercises performed in group by half of the exercisers, and the other half performs exercises in twos.

Figure 118. Exercise setting - a loose bunch, exercises performed in twos.

Figure 119. Exercise setting – a loose bunch, exercises performed in a group.

5.5. Suggestions of training settings that can be used in a warm-up with a ball and elements of tactics

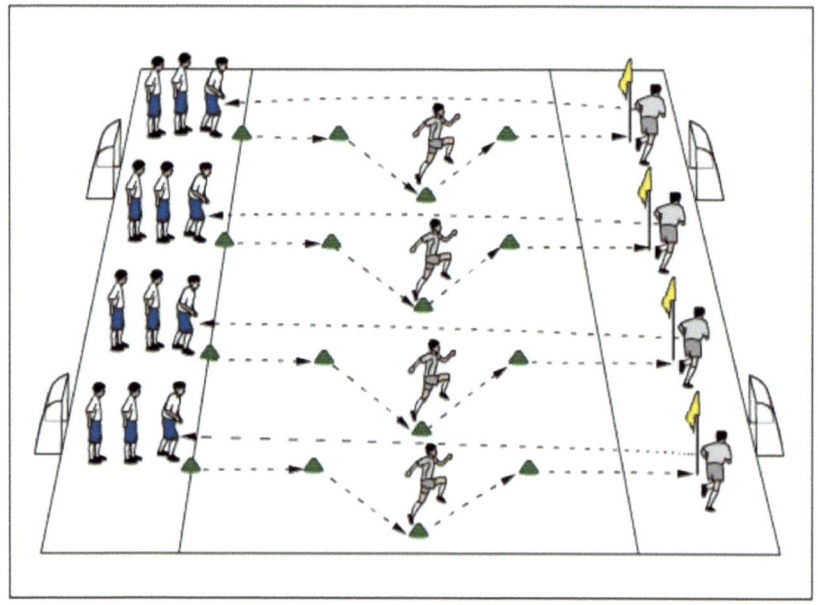

Figure 120. Exercise setting - queues, exercises performed individually by the participants.

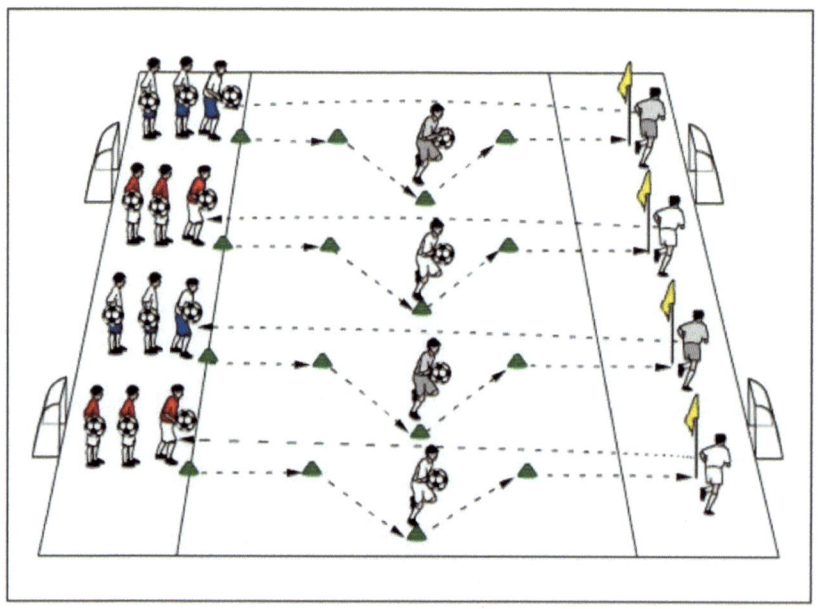

Figure 121. Exercise setting - queues, exercises performed individually by the participants.

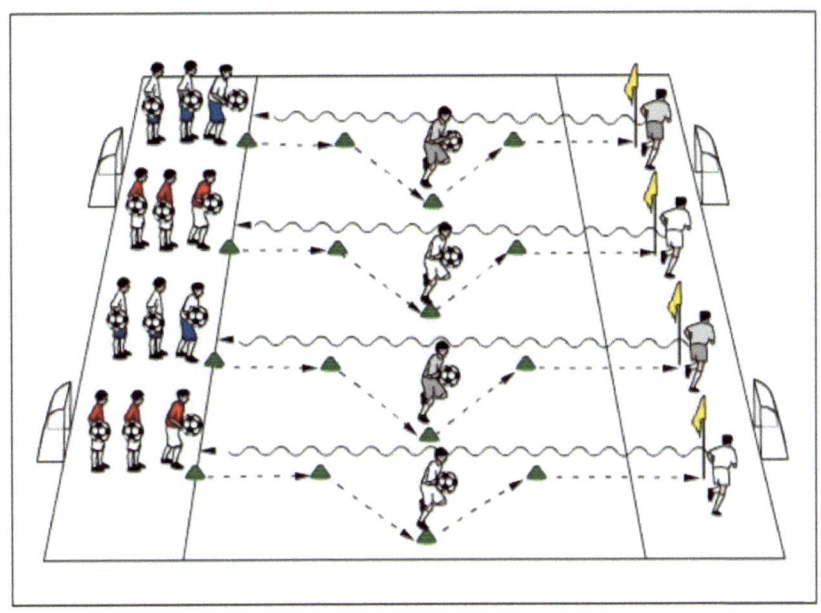

Figure 122. Exercise setting - queues, exercises performed individually by the participants.

Figure 123. Exercise setting - queues, exercises performed individually by the participants.

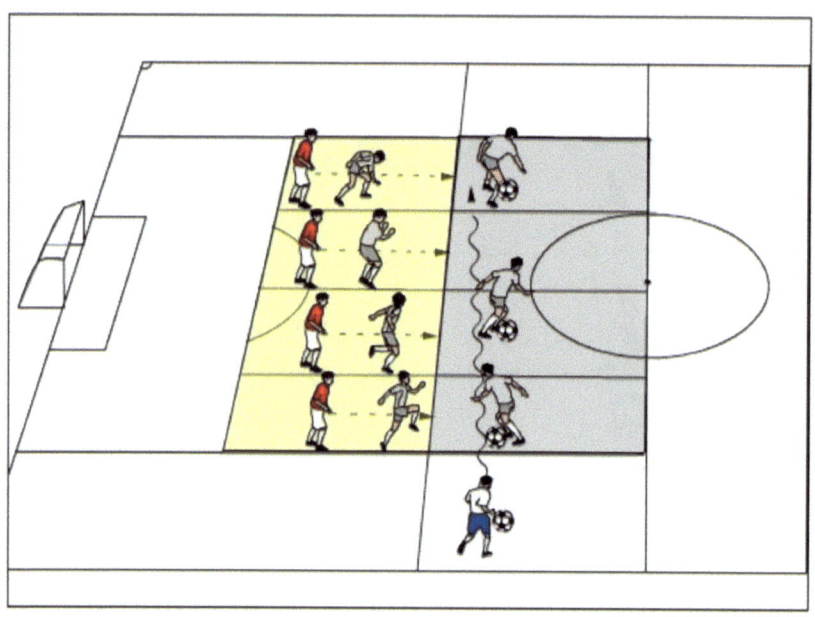

Figure 124. Exercise setting - queues, exercises performed individually by the participants.

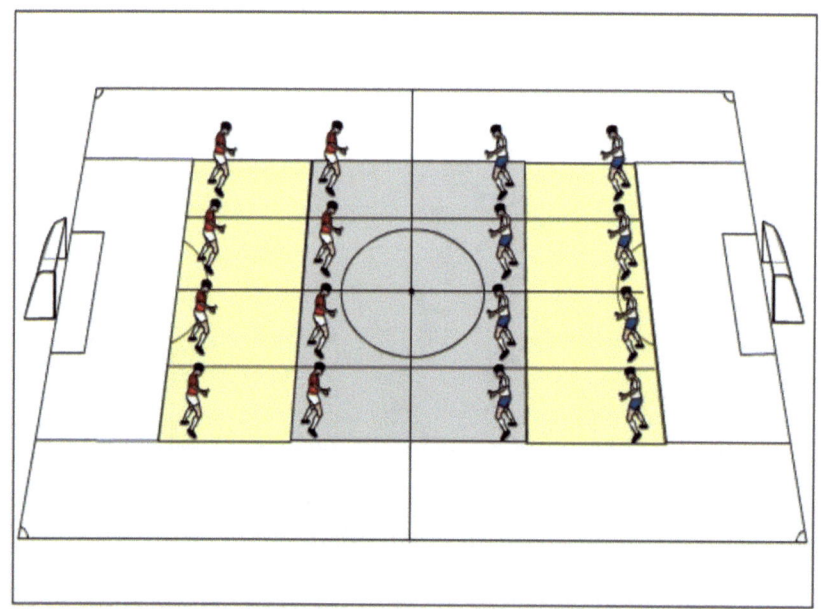

Figure 125. Exercise setting - queues, exercises performed in a group by the participants.

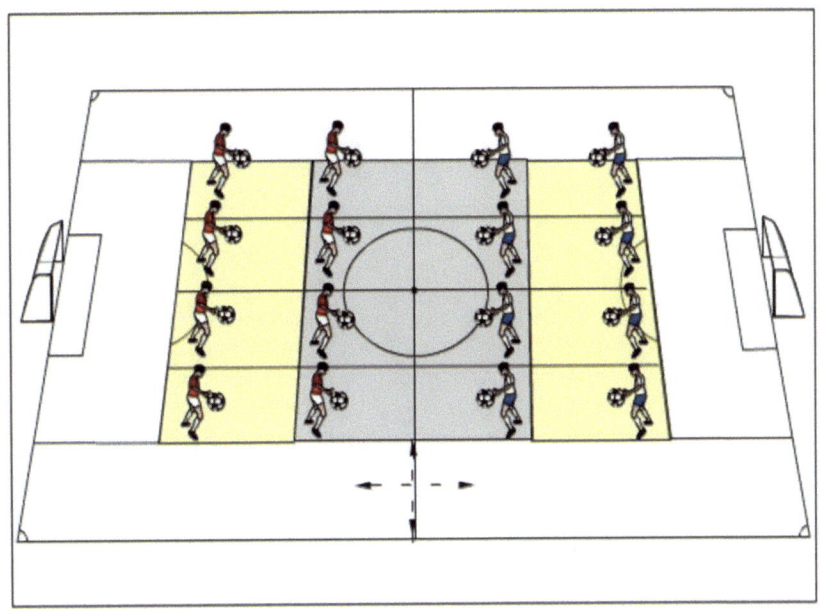

Figure 126. Exercise setting - queues, exercises performed in a group by the participants.

Figure 127. Exercise setting - queues, exercises performed in a group by the participants.

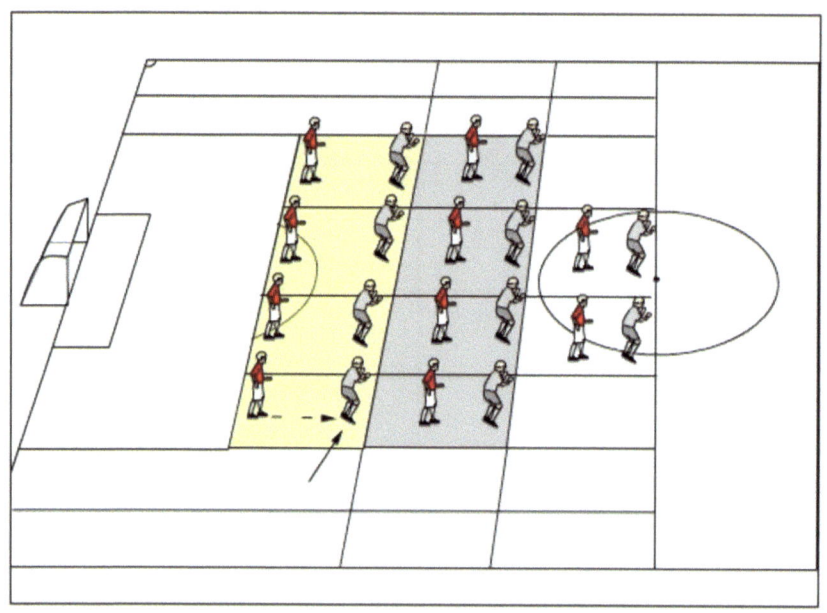

Figure 128. Exercise setting - queues, exercises performed in a group by the participants.

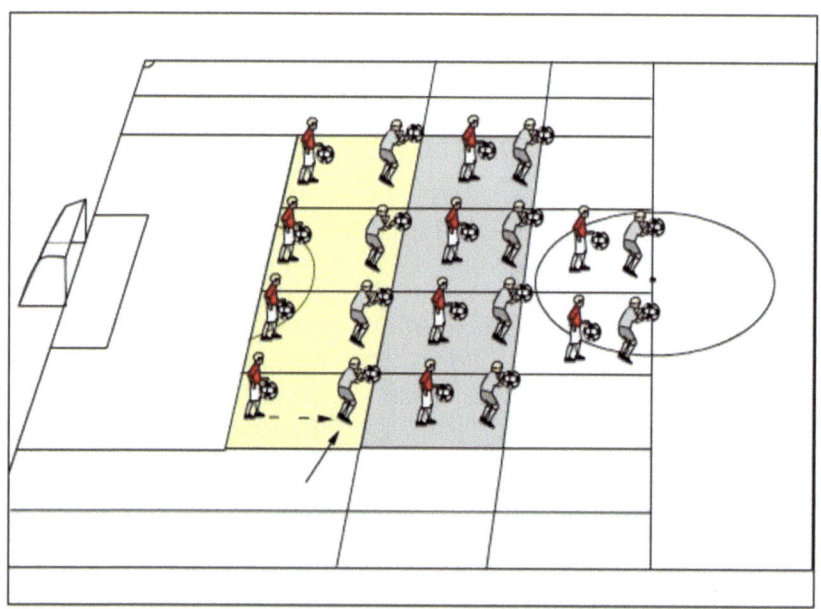

Figure 129. Exercise setting - queues, exercises performed in a group by the participants.

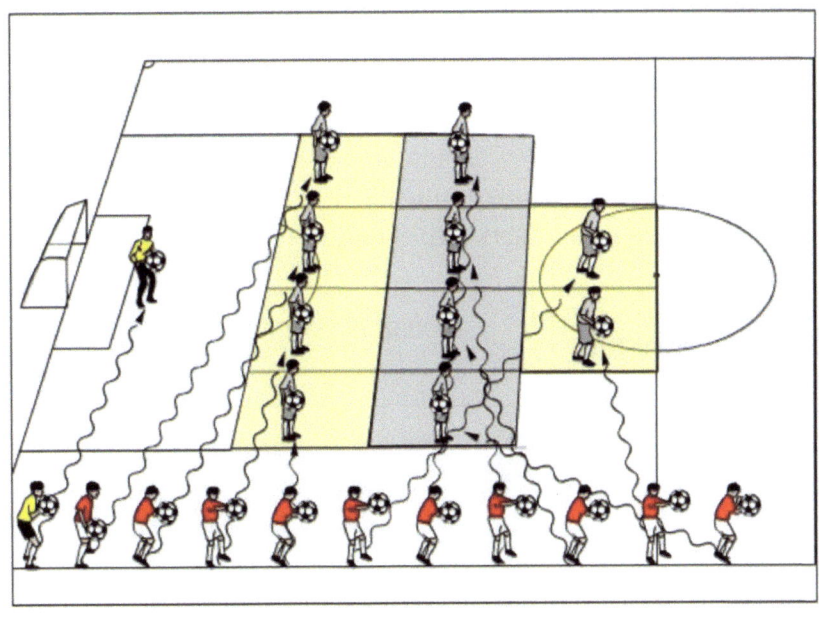

Figure 130. Exercise setting - queues, exercises performed individually by the participants.

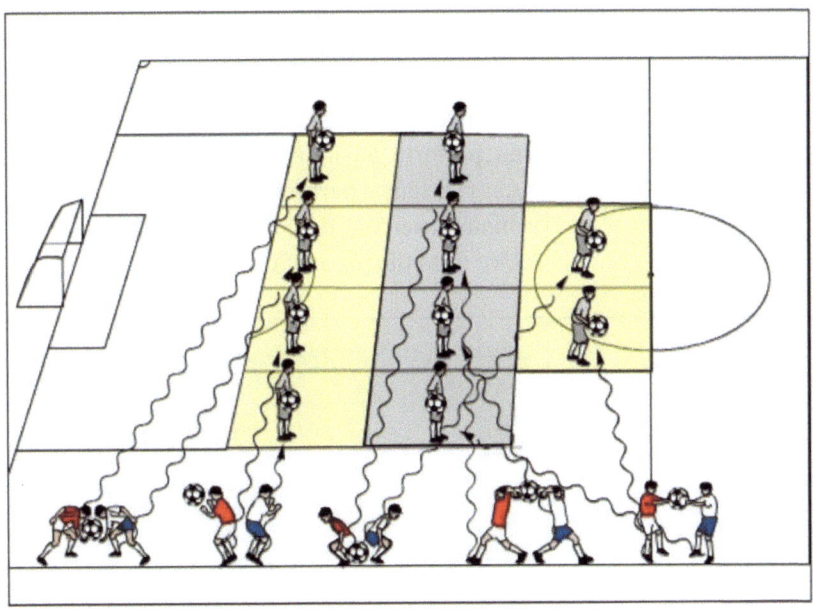

Figure 131. Exercise setting – queues, exercises performed individually by half of the exercisers, and the other half performs exercises in twos.

6. WARM-UP SCENARIOS BEFORE TRAINING SESSIONS

6.1. Scenario of a general warm-up without equipment before training sessions

\multicolumn{4}{c}{SCENARIO OF A GENERAL WARM-UP WITHOUT EQUIPMENT BEFORE TRAINING SESSIONS}
\multicolumn{4}{c}{I. SLOW RUN EXERCISES – ARMS AND LEGS EXERCISES (4').}
No.	EXERCISES DRILLS TIME / NUMBER OF REPETITIONS DIVISION OF EXERCISERS	EXERCISE SETTING	METHOD OF LEADING
1.	Shoulders S. P. – basic position – forward run towards each other and circling the arms (various forms), then return to the starting position. 1x Combined	Figure 132. Queue. Exercisers are divided into two groups A, B arranged opposite each other in queues, on the signal of the instructor, those exercising in a slow run perform an individual exercise, after reaching a partner they perform a binary exercise, then return to their place or to the place of the exerciser.	Exact
2.	Shoulders S. P. – basic position – forward run towards each other and perform a standing push up with your partner, then return to the starting position. 1x Combined	Figure 133. Queue. Exercisers are divided into two groups A, B arranged opposite each other in queues, on the signal of the instructor, those exercising in a slow	Exact

		run perform an individual exercise, after reaching a partner they perform a binary exercise, then return to their place or to the place of the exerciser.		
3.	Shoulders S. P. – basic position – forward run towards each other, jumping high five with both hands high above the head with the partner, then return to the starting position. 1x Combined	Figure 134. Queue. Exercisers are divided into two groups A, B arranged opposite each other in queues, on the signal of the instructor, those exercising in a slow run perform an individual exercise, after reaching a partner they perform a binary exercise, then return to their place or to the place of the exerciser.		Exact
4.	Shoulders S. P. – basic position – backwards run towards each other, a quarter turn and tapping the partner's shoulder, then return to the starting position (right, left shoulder). 1x Combined	Figure 135. Queue. Exercisers are divided into two groups A, B arranged opposite each other in queues, on the signal of the instructor, those exercising in a slow run perform an individual exercise, after reaching a partner they perform a binary exercise, then return to their place or to the place of the exerciser.		Exact

5.	Shoulders S. P. – basic position - running back to back along the middle, a quarter turn and tapping the partner's shoulder and running in-place. 1x Combined	Figure 136. Queue. Exercisers are divided into two groups A, B arranged opposite each other in queues, on the signal of the instructor, those exercising in a slow run perform an individual exercise, after reaching a partner they perform a binary exercise, then return to their place or to the place of the exerciser.	Exact
6.	Legs S. P. – basic position – side shuffle, side shoulders swings in the middle bypassing the partner and return to the starting position. 1x Combined	Figure 137. Queue. Exercisers are divided into two groups A, B arranged opposite each other in queues, on the signal of the instructor, those exercising in a slow run perform an individual exercise, after reaching a partner they perform a binary exercise, then return to their place or to the place of the exerciser.	Exact

7.	Legs S. P. – legs apart - side shuffle towards the centre, back to back with a partner moving in a circle, then return to the starting position. 1x Combined	Figure 138. Queue. Exercisers are divided into two groups A, B arranged opposite to each other in queues, on the signal of the instructor, those exercising in a slow run perform an individual exercise, after reaching a partner they perform a binary exercise, then return to their place or to the place of the exerciser.	Exact
8.	Legs S. P. – basic position – forward (skier) jumping jacks moving forwards towards centre, backwards run to the starting position. 1x Combined	Figure 139. Queue. Exercisers are divided into two groups A, B arranged opposite each other in queues, on the signal of the instructor, those exercising in a slow run perform an individual exercise, after reaching a partner they perform a binary exercise, then return to their place or to the place of the exerciser.	Exact

9.	Legs S. P. – basic position - skip A to the partner, squat and return to the partner's place. 1x Combined	Figure 140. Queue. Exercisers are divided into two groups A, B arranged opposite to each other in queues, on the signal of the instructor, those exercising in a slow run perform an individual exercise, after reaching a partner they perform a binary exercise, then return to their place or to the place of the exerciser.	Exact
10.	Legs S. P. – basic position – skip C to the middle, jumping chest bump with the partner, then return to partner's place. 1x Combined	Figure 141. Queue. Exercisers are divided into two groups A, B arranged opposite to each other in queues, on the signal of the instructor, those exercising in a slow run perform an individual exercise, after reaching a partner they perform a binary exercise, then return to their place or to the place of the exerciser.	Exact

11.	Legs S. P. – basic position – forwards run towards each other, around the partner and return to the starting position. 1x Combined	Figure 142. Queue. Exercisers are divided into two groups A, B arranged opposite to each other in queues, on the signal of the instructor, those exercising in a slow run perform an individual exercise, after reaching a partner they perform a binary exercise, then return to their place or to the place of the exerciser.	Exact

II. STATIONARY EXERCISES – BODY EXERCISES, ROTATIONS OF PARTICULAR JOINTS, ROTATING TOE TOUCHES ETC.

12.	Sagittal plane S. P. – basic position – forward bend with the fingertips touching the toes, then return to the starting position. 5x Individual exercises	Figure 143. Loose bunch.	Frontal
13.	Sagittal plane S. P. – sit straight, bending forwards at the hips with the fingertips touching the toes, then return to the starting position. 5x Individual exercises	Figure 144. Loose bunch.	Frontal
14.	Frontal plane S. P. – basic position, sideways bends- movement of the straight hip sideways and simultaneous		Frontal

	elevation of the opposite leg sideways, after finishing the exercise return to the starting position. 4x Individual exercises	Figure 145. Loose bunch.	
15.	Frontal plane S. P. – basic position, with arms forming an arch over the head - bend sideways, after finishing the exercise return to the starting position. 4x Individual exercises	Figure 146. Loose bunch.	Frontal
16.	Transverse plane S. P. – forward bend with the feet apart - rotations of the torso, after finishing the exercise return to the starting position. 15" Individual exercises	Figure 147. Loose bunch.	Frontal
17.	Transverse plane S. P. – position with feet apart, rotating toe touches of the right hand to the left leg and left hand to the right leg, after finishing the exercise return to the starting position. 15" Individual exercises	Figure 148. Loose bunch.	Frontal
18.	Compound plane S. P. – basic position, hip circles - extensive circular movements of the		Frontal

	hips around the vertical axis of the body, after finishing the exercise return to the starting position. 20" Individual exercises	Figure 149. Loose bunch.	
19.	Compound plane S. P. – full forward bend with the feet apart - alternate turns of the torso - after finishing the exercise return to the starting position. 20" Individual exercises	Figure 150. Loose bunch.	Frontal
III. EXERCISES PERFORMED DYNAMICALLY.			
20.	Legs S. P. – basic position - dynamic forward kicks of the right leg to the right hand and left leg to the left hand, after finishing the exercise return to the starting position. 20x Individual exercises	Figure 151. Circle.	Frontal
21.	Legs S. P. – basic position – dynamic forward kicks of the right leg to the left hand and left leg to the right hand, after finishing the exercise return to the starting position. 20x Individual exercises	Figure 152. Circle.	Frontal
22.	Legs S. P. – basic position - dynamic cross kicks of the right leg to the left hand and the left leg to the right hand,		Frontal

	after finishing the exercise return to the starting position. 20x Individual exercises	 Figure 153. Circle.	
IV. EXERCISES PERFORMED WHILE RUNNING – FAST RUN, MULTIPLE JUMPS COMBINED WITH COORDINATION EXERCISES.			
23.	Legs S. P. – basic position, fast run towards each other, hold hands, full turn and run in - place, then return to the starting position. 1x Combined	Figure 154. Queue.	Mixed
24.	Legs S. P. – basic position, fast run towards each other, hold hands, full turn and run to your partner's place, then return to the starting position. 1x Combined	Figure 155. Queue.	Mixed
25.	Legs S. P. – basic position, running towards each other, crawling through the partner's legs and running to his place, then return to the starting position. 1x Combined	Figure 156. Queue.	Mixed

26.	Legs S. P. – basic position, fast run towards each other, imitation of a jumping header, running in - place, then return to the starting position. 1x Combined	Figure 157. Queue.	Mixed
27.	Legs S. P. – basic position, fast run towards each other, burpee, run to the partner's place, then return to the starting position. 1x Combined	Figure 158. Queue.	Mixed
28.	Legs S. P. – basic position, jumping forwards on the right leg towards each other, skipping A in place for 3 seconds, first, they jump on the right leg facing each other, they stop in the middle, perform skipping A for 3 seconds and jump back to the starting position on the left leg. 1x Combined	Figure 159. Queue.	Mixed
29.	Legs S. P. – basic position, two footed forward hops, "synchronous jumping jacks for 10 seconds", Two-footed hops back to the starting position. 1x Combined	Figure 160. Queue.	Mixed

	V. DYNAMIC OR STATIC STRETCHING EXERCISES.		
30.	Legs S. P. – a) tension: standing on one leg, bend the other leg in the knee joint and grasp the foot (left leg - left hand), push the foot down against the hand trying to overcome the resistance. b) relaxation. c) stretching: bend the leg in the knee joint and grasp the foot with your hand, then lead the leg back up until the heel touches the buttocks. 1x LL & RL Individual exercises	Figure 161. Circle.	Frontal
31.	Legs S. P. – a) tension: kneel on one knee, straighten the other leg diagonally, rest the heel on the ground, firmly press into the ground with the straight leg. b) relaxation. c) stretching: in the same position with the back as straight as possible, forward bend. 1x LL & RL Individual exercises	Figure 162. Circle.	Frontal
32.	Legs S. P. – a) tension: standing, feet wide apart, press your feet down inwards, putting pressure on the ground. b) relaxation. c) stretching: stand with legs apart as wide as possible, and stay in this position. 1x Individual exercises	Figure 163. Circle.	Frontal
	VI. COORDINATION EXERCISES PERFORMED WITH A PARTNER.		
33.	Shoulders Legs S. P. – basic position, exerciser number 1 - hops on both feet with alternate arm circulation (e.g. left hand forward, right hand backward, freely changing) moving in any direction, exerciser number 2 imitates number 1 standing in front of him (so-called mirror image), on	Figure 164. Loose bunch.	Frontal

	the coach's signal changing of the exercise leader, after finishing the exercise return to the starting position. 1' Binary exercises		
34.	Shoulders Legs S. P. – basic position, feet apart, exerciser No. 1 - both feet jumps with a simultaneous rise of arms sideways clapping, moving in any directions (jamping jacks), exerciser No. 2 imitates exerciser No. 1 standing in front of him (so-called mirror reflection), on the signal - change of the exercise leader, after finishing the exercise return to the starting position. 1' Binary exercises	Figure 165. Loose bunch.	Frontal
35.	Shoulders Legs S. P. – Exerciser No. 1 doing a sit - up - performs sideways rotations by pushing his hands away from the ground, exerciser No. 2 in basic position, jumps over the partner's legs, on the signal change of the exercise leader, after finishing the exercise return to the starting position. 1,5' Binary exercises	Figure 166. Loose bunch.	Frontal
36.	Shoulders Legs S. P. – basic position, exerciser No. 1 - performs any coordination exercises while simultaneously engaging arms and legs, moving in any directions, exerciser No. 2 imitates the exerciser No. 1 standing in front of him (so-called mirror reflection), on the signal, change of the exercise leader, after finishing the exercise return to the starting position.	Figure 167. Loose bunch.	Individual

No.	1' Binary exercises		

6.2. Scenario of a general warm-up with equipment other than a ball before training sessions

SCENARIO OF A GENERAL WARM-UP WITH EQUIPMENT OTHER THAN A BALL BEFORE TRAINING SESSIONS			
I. SLOW RUN EXERCISES – ARMS AND LEGS EXERCISES.			
No.	EXERCISES DRILLS TIME / NUMBER OF REPETITIONS DIVISION OF EXERCISERS	EXERCISE SETTING	METHOD OF LEADING	TEACHING MEASURES
1.	Shoulders S. P. – basic position - a slow run, stick at chest height, wide grip then raising stick with one hand: slow run combined with moving the stick from the right to the left hand, after finishing the exercise return to the starting position. 10x Individual exercises	Figure 168. Circle.	Frontal	Gymnastic stick
2.	Shoulders S. P. – basic position - a slow run, stick on the shoulders, wide grip, pull up with both hands: a slow run combined with sliding the stick to the right and left, after finishing the exercise return to the starting position. 10x Individual exercises	Figure 169. Circle.	Frontal	Gymnastic stick

3.	Shoulders S. P. – basic position - a slow run, stick on the shoulders, wide grip, pull up with both hands: slow running combined with the stick rising up and the shoulder drop, after finishing the exercise return to the starting position. 10x Individual exercises	Figure 170. Circle.	Frontal	Gymnastic stick
4.	Shoulders S. P. – basic position - a slow run, stick on the back at the level of the hips, wide grip pull up with both hands: slow run with the stick rising up and down, after finishing the exercise return to the starting position. 10x Individual exercises	Figure 171. Circle.	Frontal	Gymnastic stick
5.	Legs S. P. – basic position - a slow run, hold the stick with your hands at chest height: slow run combined with rhythmic raising of the knee of the left leg, and then the right leg (every third step), after finishing the exercise return to the starting position. 10x Individual exercises	Figure 172. Circle.	Frontal	Gymnastic stick
6.	Legs S. P. – basic position - a slow run, hold the stick with your hands at the height of the chest, slow run combined with a forward lunge every 3rd step on the left leg, then the right leg, with the arms raised with	Figure 173. Circle.	Frontal	Gymnastic stick

	the stick above the head, after finishing the exercise return to the starting position. 10x Individual exercises			
7.	Legs and trunk S. P. – basic position - a slow run, at the instructor's signal, partner up and run into the circle, one partner lying on his back, legs straight and together, raised at a 45° angle. The other partner in the kneeling position holds a stick above the partner's legs: the partner makes circles around the stick with his legs joined together and straight, after finishing the exercise return to the starting position. 15x Combined	Figure 174. Circle.	Frontal	Gymnastic stick
8.	Legs and trunk S. P. – basic position - a slow run, on the signal of the instructor, the players get in pairs and run into the circle, lie down, legs apart, raised at a 45° angle. The partner exercising in the kneeling position holds a stick above his partner's legs: legs apart then joined above the stick, after finishing the exercise return to the starting position. 15x Combined	Figure 175. Circle.	Frontal	Gymnastic stick

	II. STATIONARY EXERCISES – BODY EXERCISES, ROTATIONS OF PARTICULAR JOINTS, ROTATING TOE TOUCHES ETC.			
9.	Transverse plane S. P. – basic position - arms forward holding a hula hoop with both hands, torso rotates smoothly from one side to the other, after finishing the exercise return to the starting position. 10x Individual exercises	Figure 176. Loose bunch.	Frontal	Hula Hoop
10.	Compound plane S. P. – basic position - hula hoop held at hip level, circulation of the torso, we set the hips in motion, making circular movements spinning the hula hoop, after a minute change direction, after finishing the exercise return to the starting position. 2' Individual exercises	Figure 177. Loose bunch.	Frontal	Hula Hoop
11.	Sagittal plane S. P. – basic position, arms forward holding a hula hoop with both hands, bend forward, after finishing the exercise back to the starting position. 10x Individual exercises	Figure 178. Loose bunch.	Frontal	Hula Hoop
12.	Frontal plane S. P. – basic position, arms up holding a hula hoop with both hands, bend sideways, after finishing the exercise back to the starting position. 10x Individual exercises	Figure 179. Loose bunch.	Frontal	Hula Hoop

13.	Sagittal plane S. P. – basic position - arms down holding a hula hoop with both hands, bent knees, forward lean, we extend the hula hoop forwards as far as possible leaning it on the floor, after finishing the exercise return to the starting position. 10x Individual exercises	Figure 180. Loose bunch.	Frontal	Hula hoop
14.	Sagittal plane S. P. - sitting down straight, holding a hula hoop forward with both hands, bend forwards as far as possible, after finishing the exercise return to the starting position. 10x Individual exercises	Figure 181. Loose bunch.	Frontal	Hula Hoop
15.	Sagittal plane S. P. – basic position - arms down holding a hula hoop with both hands, bent knees, lean forwards, we extend the hula hoop forward as far as possible leaning it against the floor, after finishing the exercise return to the starting position. 10x Individual exercises	Figure 182. Loose bunch.	Frontal	Hula hoop
16.	Transverse plane S. P. – sit straight, in twos, with their backs to each other, holding a hula hoop forward with both hands - torso turns with the hula hoop to the partner, after finishing the exercise return to the starting position. 20x Binary exercises	Figure 183. Loose bunch.	Frontal	Hula hoop

17.	Sagittal plane S. P. – sit straight, in twos, with their backs to each other, a hula hoop is held with both hands - the hula hoop above the head, bend forward with the hula hoop, after finishing the exercise return to the starting position. 20x Binary exercises	Figure 184. Loose bunch.	Frontal	Hula Hoop
	III. DYNAMIC STRETCHING EXERCISES.			
18.	Legs S. P. – basic position - sideways position towards the ladder, grip the ladder with the left hand at shoulder height, the right leg with extensive circulation in the hip joint forwards and then backwards, then the same for the left leg, after finishing the exercise return to the starting position. 10x RL forward 10x RL backwards 10x LL forward 10x LL backwards Individual exercises	Figure 185. Loose bunch.	Frontal	Gymnastic ladder
19.	Legs S. P. – basic position - facing the ladder, hold the ladder with both hands at shoulder height, left leg extensive swings in the hip joint to the side, then the same for the right leg, after finishing the exercise return to the starting position. 10x RL to the side 10x LL to the side Individual exercises	Figure 186. Loose bunch.	Frontal	Gymnastic ladder

20.	Legs S. P. – basic position - sideways towards the ladder, the left hand grabs a rung at shoulder height, the right leg swings forward and then backwards, then the same for the left leg, after finishing the exercise return to the starting position. 10x RL forward 10x RL backwards 10x LL forward 10x LL backward Individual exercises	Figure 187. Loose bunch.		Frontal	Gymnastic ladder

IV. EXERCISES PERFORMED WHILE RUNNING – FAST RUN, MULTIPLE JUMPS COMBINED WITH COORDINATION EXERCISES.

21.	Shoulders Legs S. P. – basic position - arms down holding the skipping rope, one signal, two-foot skipping while moving forward, two signals move backwards, three signals move to the right, four signals move to the left, after finishing the exercise return to the starting position. 1' Individual exercises	Figure 188. Loose bunch.		Frontal	Skipping rope
22.	Shoulders Legs S. P. – basic position -arms down holding the skipping rope with both hands, one signal alternating one - leg skipping moving forward, two signals moving backwards, three signals moving to the right, four signals moving to the left, after finishing the exercise, return to the starting position.	Figure 189. Loose bunch.		Frontal	Skipping rope

	1' Individual exercises			
23.	Shoulders Legs S. P. – basic position - arms down holding the skipping rope, one signal skipping on the right leg moving forward, two signals moving backwards on the left leg, three signals - skipping on the right leg moving to the right, four signals skipping on the left leg moving to the left, after finishing the exercise return to the starting position. 1' Individual exercises	Figure 190. Loose bunch.	Frontal	Skipping rope
24.	Shoulders Legs S. P. – basic position - arms down holding the rope, skipping at a very fast pace for 15", then the trainees get in pairs and do any exercise, after finishing the exercise return to the starting position. 1' Combined	Figure 191. Loose bunch.	Individual	Skipping rope
V. DYNAMIC OR STATIC STRETCHING EXERCISES.				
25.	Legs S. P. – straddle position, slowly moving forward with legs wide apart along the mattress without touching it with the feet, after finishing the exercise return to the starting position. 10x Individual exercises	Figure 192. Loose bunch.	Frontal	Gym mattress

26.	Legs S. P. – kneeling, slow backward bend, holding this position for 5 seconds, after finishing the exercise return to the starting position. 10x Individual exercises	Figure 193. Loose bunch.	Frontal	Gym mattress
27.	Legs S. P. – sit with your legs apart facing your partner, hold hands, pull and push the partner's hands, after finishing the exercise return to the starting position. 30" Binary exercises	Figure 194. Loose bunch.	Frontal	Gym mattress
VI. COORDINATION EXERCISES WITH ACCESSORIES.				
28.	Legs S. P. – basic position, step forward with the left leg (standing above the rung) jump and change legs so that the right leg is ahead (standing over the next rung), after finishing the exercise return to the starting position. 4x Individual exercises	Figure 195. Queue.	Frontal	Agility ladder
29.	Legs S. P. – basic position, step forward with the left leg (standing above the rung) while jumping change legs so that the right leg is ahead (standing over the same rung), then jump and change the legs over the next rung - when jumping over the next rung, the same leg is always ahead, after finishing the exercise return to the starting position. 4x	Figure 196. Queue.	Frontal	Agility ladder

	Individual exercises			
30.	Legs S. P. – basic position, standing astride over the side straps of the ladder, two foot jump from the left side of the strap to the right side over the next rung, after finishing the exercise return to the starting position. 4x Individual exercises	Figure 197. Queue.	Frontal	Agility ladder

6.3. Scenario of a general warm-up with a ball before training

SCENARIO OF A GENERAL WARM-UP WITH A BALL BEFORE TRAINING					
I. SLOW RUN EXERCISES – ARMS AND LEGS EXERCISES.					
No.	EXERCISES DRILLS TIME / NUMBER OF REPETITIONS DIVISION OF EXERCISERS	EXERCISE SETTING	METHOD OF DRIBBLING	TEACHING AIDS
1.	Arms S. P. – basic position - slow running, alternate arm circles forwards, between ball throws, after finishing the exercise return to the starting position. 20' Individual exercises	Figure 198. Queue.	Frontal	Ball
2.	Arms S. P. – basic position - slow running, simultaneous forward arm circles, between ball throws, after finishing the exercise return to the starting position. 30' Individual exercises	Figure 199. Loose bunch.	Frontal	Ball

3.	Arms S. P. – basic position - slow running, alternate arm circles backwards, between ball throws, after finishing the exercise return to the starting position. 20' Individual exercises	Figure 200. Loose bunch.	Frontal	Ball
4.	Arms S. P. – basic position - slow running, simultaneous backward arm circles, between ball throws, after finishing the exercise return to the starting position. 30' Individual exercises	Figure 201. Loose bunch.	Frontal	Ball
5.	Arms S. P. – basic position - slow running, tossing the ball over the head back and forth from the left hand to the right hand, after finishing the exercise return to the starting position. 20' Individual exercises	Figure 202. Loose bunch.	Frontal	Ball
6.	Legs S. P. – basic position - slow running dribbling the ball, on the signal stop the ball by sitting on it, then return to the starting position. 30' Individual exercises	Figure 203. Loose bunch.	Frontal	Ball
7.	Legs S. P. – basic position - slow running, dribbling the ball, on the signal stop the ball with the sole and performing both two-foot jumps over the ball, then return to the starting position. 30' Individual exercises	Figure 204. Loose bunch.	Frontal	Ball

8.	Legs S. P. – basic position - slow running, ball in the right hand, alternating leg lifts with a bent knee passing the ball underneath from the outside, alternately under the right and left legs, after finishing the exercise return to the starting position. 20' Individual exercises	Figure 205. Loose bunch.	Frontal	Ball
9.	Legs S. P. – basic position - slow run, ball in the right hand, alternating leg lifts with a bent knee, the ball passing underneath the leg from the inside, alternately under the right and left legs, after finishing the exercise return to the starting position. 20' Individual exercises	Figure 206. Loose bunch.	Frontal	Ball
10.	Legs S. P. – basic position - slow running dribbling the ball with the left foot, at the signal of the leader changing to the right leg, after finishing the exercise return to the starting position. 20' Individual exercises	Figure 207. Loose bunch.	Frontal	Ball
II. STATIONARY EXERCISES – BODY EXERCISES, ROTATIONS OF PARTICULAR JOINTS, ROTATING TOE TOUCHES ETC.				
11.	Sagittal plane S. P. – lying on the stomach – holding the ball in the hands, throw the ball up, sit up, then quickly stand and catch the ball with both hands, after finishing the exercise return to the starting position. 10x Individual exercises	Figure 208. Loose bunch.	Frontal	Ball

12.	Sagittal plane S. P. – lying on the stomach - arms up with the ball held in both hands, lean the torso back as much as possible, after finishing the exercise return to the starting position. 20' Individual exercises	Figure 209. Loose bunch.	Frontal	Ball
13.	Transverse plane S. P. – straddle position - raise arms forward with the ball held in both hands, rotate to the right and left, after finishing the exercise return to starting position. 20' Individual exercises	Figure 210. Loose bunch.	Frontal	Ball
14.	Compound plane S. P. – straddle position – arms raised holding the ball, perform hip circles, after finishing the exercise return to the starting position. 20' 10 to the right 10 to the left Individual exercises	Figure 211. Loose bunch.	Frontal	Ball
15.	Compound plane S. P. – straddle position - arms down holding the ball, between the legs (left hand behind the left leg, right hand in front of the right leg), bent forward, release the grip of the ball and grab it again before it falls to the ground after changing hands (right hand behind the right leg, left hand in front of the left leg), after finishing the exercise return to the starting position. 20' Individual exercises	Figure 212. Loose bunch.	Frontal	Ball

16.	Sagittal plane S. P. – basic position - hands down holding the ball, throw the ball vertically upwards, bend forward and touch the toes, stand up and jump, catching the falling ball, then return to the starting position. 20x Individual exercises	Figure 213. Loose bunch.	Frontal	Ball
17.	Sagittal plane S. P. – basic position - arms up, bent forward with the ball touching the ground, roll the ball between the legs in a figure eight, after finishing the exercise return to the starting position. 20x Individual exercises	Figure 214. Loose bunch.	Frontal	Ball
18.	Compound plane S. P. – straddle position, arms up holding the ball with both hands, lean back, release the ball, rotate once to the right, once to the left and catch the bouncing ball, then return to the starting position. 20' Individual exercises	Figure 215. Loose bunch.	Frontal	Ball
19.	Sagittal plane S.P. – lie down on the back– holding the ball in the hands, throw the ball up, sit up, and catch the ball, then return to the starting position. 20x Individual exercises	Figure 216. Loose bunch.	Frontal	Ball
III. DYNAMIC FLEXIBILITY EXERCISES.				
20.	Legs S. P. – basic position - arms up holding the ball with both hands, in - place, dynamic alternating kicks of the legs straightened at the knee with simultaneous swinging of the	Figure 217. Loose bunch.	Frontal	Ball

	arms forward so that the ball touches the raised leg, after finishing the exercise return to the starting position. 30' Individual exercises			
21.	Legs S. P. – basic position - the ball in the right hand, dynamic alternating kicks of the legs straightened at the knee with the ball passed underneath from the inside, with a simultaneous jump on the standing leg, after finishing the exercise return to the starting position. 30' Individual exercises	Figure 218. Loose bunch.	Frontal	Ball
22.	Legs S. P. – straddle position - arms up holding the ball with both hands, bend forwards touching the ground in front of the feet once on the right, once on the left side, after finishing the exercise return to the starting position. 15x RL 15x LL Individual exercises	Figure 219. Loose bunch.	Frontal	Ball
IV. DYNAMIC EXERCISES PERFORMED WHILE RUNNING – FAST RUN, MULTIPLE JUMPS COMBINED WITH COORDINATION EXERCISES.				
23.	Shoulders Legs S. P. – basic position - arms up with both hands holding the ball, strong throw of the ball against the ground, catching the ball after a bounce with the laces, then 10 jumps forwards and backwards over the ball, then return to the starting position. 10x Individual exercises	Figure 220. Loose bunch.	Frontal	Ball

24.	Shoulders Legs S. P. – basic position - the ball is between the feet, two foot jumps with high knees holding the ball between the feet, after finishing the exercise return to the starting position. 15″ Individual exercises	Figure 221. Loose bunch.	Frontal	Ball
25.	Shoulders Legs S. P. – basic position - arms up with both hands holding the ball, strong throw of the ball against the ground, trapping the ball after a bounce with the laces, then push up position on the ball, 2 push ups, then return to the starting position. 10x Individual exercises	Figure 222. Loose bunch.	Frontal	Ball
26.	Shoulders Legs S. P. – basic position – ball between the feet, launch the ball upwards with the feet, jump and catch the ball, then return to the starting position. 12x Individual exercises	Figure 223. Loose bunch.	Frontal	Ball
27.	Shoulders Legs S. P. – basic position - arms down holding the ball with both hands, throw the ball upwards at a distance of about 1 m, catch the ball with both hands after bouncing at the lowest possible point, then return to the starting position. 10x Individual exercises	Figure 224. Loose bunch.	Frontal	Ball

28.	Shoulders Legs S. P. – basic position - arms down holding the ball with both hands, throw the ball forward at a distance of about 4m, sprint to the ball and catch with both hands, then return to the starting position. 10x Individual exercises	Figure 225. Loose bunch.	Frontal	Ball
	V. DYNAMIC OR STATIC FLEXIBILITY EXERCISES.			
29.	Legs S. P. – basic position - arms forward with both hands holding the ball, forward lunge alternating leading foot with the ball simultaneously touching the knee of the lunging leg, after finishing the exercise return to the starting position. 12x Individual exercises	Figure 226. Loose bunch.	Frontal	Ball
30.	Legs S. P. – basic position - alternate side lunge, rolling the ball with the hands around the foot, after finishing the exercise return to the starting position. 6xLL 6xRL Individual exercises	Figure 227. Loose bunch.	Frontal	Ball
31.	Legs S. P. - straight straddle sit, hands down holding the ball, rolling the ball with both hands on the ground around the body, after finishing the exercise return to the starting position. 12x Individual exercises	Figure 228. Loose bunch.	Frontal	Ball

32.	Legs S. P. – lying on the back - arms to the side, ball in the right hand, raising the left leg and bringing the foot to the ball in the right hand on the ground, take the ball with the left hand and repeat the exercise for the right leg, after finishing the exercise return to the starting position. 10xLL 10xRL Individual exercises	Figure 229. Loose bunch.	Frontal	Ball
VI. COORDINATION EXERCISES WITH A BALL.				
33.	Shoulders Legs S. P. – basic position - alternate passing of the ball with the arms and legs, exerciser A has the ball in his hands, performs a pass with both hands from behind the head (technique used just like throw-in from the side-line) to exerciser B, who at the same time passes the ball with the inner part of the foot to exerciser A, after finishing the exercise return to the starting position. 1' Binary exercises	Figure 230. Queue. Exercisers are divided into two groups A, B across from each other, each student has two balls and at the signal of the instructor performs specific individual or binary exercises with two balls, then they return to their place or to the place of their partner.	Frontal	Ball
34.	Shoulders Legs S. P. – basic position - running forwards and backwards, alternate passes by the exercisers with their arms and legs, exerciser A has the ball in his hands, passes with both hands from the front of the chest to exerciser B, who at the same time passes the ball with the inner part of the	Figure 231. Queue. Exercisers are divided into two groups A, B across from each other, each student has	Frontal	Ball

	foot to exerciser A, after finishing the exercise return to the starting position. 1' Binary exercises	two balls and at the signal of the instructor performs specific individual or binary exercises with two balls, then they return to their place or to the place of their partner.		
35.	Shoulders Legs S. P. – basic position - running forwards and backwards, alternate passes of the ball with the arms and legs, exerciser A has the ball in his hands, performs a pass with both hands in front of the chest with a bounce to exerciser B, who simultaneously passes the ball with the inner part of the foot to exerciser A, after finishing the exercise return to the starting position. 1' Binary exercises	Figure 232. Queue. Exercisers are divided into two groups A, B across from each other, each student has two balls and at the signal of the instructor performs specific individual or binary exercises with two balls, then they return to their place or to the place of their partner.	Frontal	Ball
36.	Shoulders Legs S. P. – basic position - simultaneous pass of two balls with the help of hands and legs by the exercisers, exercisers A and B have the ball in their hands and on the ground in front of their feet, they perform simultaneous passes with both their hands in front of the chest, and with the inner part of their foot, after finishing the exercise return to the starting position. 1' Binary exercises	Figure 233. Queue. Exercisers are divided into two groups A, B across from each other, each student has two balls and at the signal of the instructor performs specific individual or binary exercises with two balls, then they return to their place or to the place of their partner.	Frontal	Ball

37.	Legs S. P. – basic position - there are two balls on the ground in front of the exerciser, simultaneous dribbling of two balls with any method the exerciser chooses, after finishing the exercise return to the starting position. 1' Individual exercises	Figure 234. Queue. Exercisers are divided into two groups A, B across from each other, each student has two balls and at the signal of the instructor performs specific individual or binary exercises with two balls, then they return to their place or to the place of their partner.	Frontal	Ball
38.	Shoulders Legs S. P. – basic position - there is one ball on the ground in front of the exerciser and another in his hands, simultaneously dribbling the ball with the leading leg, using any method, and circling the other ball around the torso, after finishing the exercise return to the starting position. 1' Individual exercises	Figure 235. Queue. Exercisers are divided into two groups A, B across from each other, each student has two balls and at the signal of the instructor performs specific individual or binary exercises with two balls, then they return to their place or to the place of their partner.	Frontal	Ball
39.	Shoulders Legs S. P. – basic position - there is one ball, on the ground in front of the exerciser and another in his hands, simultaneously dribbling the ball with the leading leg, using any method, and dribbling the second ball with	Figure 236. Queue. Exercisers are divided into two groups A, B across from	Frontal	Ball

	the opposite hand, after finishing the exercise return to the starting position. 1' Individual exercises	each other, each student has two balls and at the signal of the instructor performs specific individual or binary exercises with two balls, then they return to their place or to the place of their partner.		
40.	Legs S. P. – basic position - exercisers at a distance of about 1.5m from each other, both exercisers juggle the ball with their legs at the same time, at the signal of the leader they exchange balls between them without allowing them to fall to the ground, after finishing the exercise return to the starting position. 1' Individual exercises	Figure 237. Queue. Exercisers are divided into two groups A, B across from of each other, each student has two balls and at the signal of the instructor performs specific individual or binary exercises with two balls, then they return to their place or to the place of their partner.	Frontal	Ball

6.4. Ball-oriented warm-up scenarios and special technique elements before training sessions

\multicolumn{5}{c}{DIRECTED WARM-UP SCENARIO WITH A BALL AND SPECIAL TECHNIQUES BEFORE TRAINING SESSIONS}
\multicolumn{5}{c}{I. SLOW RUN EXERCISES – ARMS AND LEGS EXERCISES.}
No.	EXERCISES DRILLS TIME – NUMBER OF REPETITIONS DIVISION OF EXERCISERS	EXERCISE SETTING	METHOD OF DRIBBLING	TEACHING AIDS
1.	Shoulders S. P. – basic position - slow run, alternating forward arm circles while leading the ball with the sole of the foot in different directions, after finishing the exercise return to the starting position. 20' Individual exercises	Figure 238. Loose bunch.	Frontal	Ball
2.	Shoulders S. P. – basic position - slow run, forward arm circles while leading the ball with the sole of the foot in different directions, after finishing the exercise return to the starting position. 30' Individual exercises	Figure 239. Loose bunch.	Frontal	Ball
3.	Shoulders S. P. – basic position - slow run, alternating backward arm circles while leading the ball with the sole of the foot in different directions, after finishing the exercise return to the starting position. 20' Individual exercises	Figure 240. Loose bunch.	Frontal	Ball

4.	Shoulders S. P. – basic position - slow run, backwards arms circles leading the ball with the sole of the foot in different directions, after finishing the exercise return to the starting position. 30' Individual exercises	Figure 241. Loose bunch.	Frontal	Ball
5.	Shoulders S. P. – basic position - slow run, hand behind the ball, one handed overhead throw, catch the ball with the other hand to return to the starting position. 20' Individual exercises	Figure 242. Loose bunch.	Frontal	Ball
6.	Legs S. P. – basic position - slow run, dribbling, on the signal of the leader, switching to juggling with the feet, after finishing the exercise return to the starting position. 30' Individual exercises	Figure 243. Loose bunch.	Frontal	Ball
7.	Legs S. P. – basic position - slow run, dribbling, on the signal of the leader, stopping the ball with the sole of the foot and performing alternating jumps with the sole touching the ball, after finishing the exercise return to the starting position. 30' Individual exercises	Figure 244. Loose bunch.	Frontal	Ball
8.	Legs S. P. – basic position - slow run, alternate thigh juggling on the signal of the leader, after finishing the exercise return to the starting position. 30'	Figure 245. Loose bunch.	Frontal	Ball

	Individual exercises			
9.	Legs S. P. – basic position - slow run, ball in the right hand, alternate bent leg rises with the ball passing underneath the leg from the outside, alternately on the right and left, after finishing the exercise return to the starting position. 20' Individual exercises	Figure 246. Loose bunch.	Frontal	Ball
10.	Legs S. P. – basic position - slow run, on the signal of the leader, forward lunges alternating legs with the ball in the hands, after finishing the exercise return to the starting position. 20' Individual exercises	Figure 247. Loose bunch.	Frontal	Ball
II. STATIONARY EXERCISES – BODY EXERCISES, ROTATIONS OF PARTICULAR JOINTS, ROTATING TOE TOUCHES ETC.				
11.	Sagittal plane S. P. – straddle position - raise arms with the ball, lean back with maximum extension of the hips forward - throw the ball behind to bounce off the ground so that it bounces between the legs and returns from the front of the exerciser, then return to the starting position. 15x Individual exercises	Figure 248. Loose bunch.	Frontal	Ball
12.	Frontal plane S. P. – straddle position - raising the left arm to the side, the ball in the right hand, lean the torso to the side with the transfer of the ball from the right hand to the left hand,	Figure 249. Loose bunch.	Frontal	Ball

	then return to the starting position. 20' Individual exercises			
13.	Transverse plane S. P. – straddle position - raising the arms forward, the ball in the right hand, torso turns with the transfer of the ball from the right hand to the left hand, then return to the starting position. 20' Individual exercises	Figure 250. Loose bunch.	Frontal	Ball
14.	Compound plane S. P. – straddle position - raising the arms holding the ball, hip circles, after finishing the exercise return to the starting position. 20' 10 to the right side 10 to the left side Individual exercises	Figure 251. Loose bunch.	Frontal	Ball
15.	Compound plane S. P. – straddle position - arms down holding the ball, bending forwards at the hips, roll the ball on the ground in figure eights around the right leg and left leg, then return to the starting position. 20' Individual exercises	Figure 252. Loose bunch.	Frontal	Ball
16.	Sagittal plane S. P. – basic position - arms down holding the ball, throwing the ball vertically upwards, bending forwards at the hips to touch the toes, stand up and catch the ball, then return to the starting position. 20x Individual exercises	Figure 253. Loose bunch.	Frontal	Ball

17.	Sagittal plane S. P. – lying back - arms up, the ball is between the legs, raise the chest and bring the hands to touch the ball, then lower the chest, return to the starting position. 20x Individual exercises	Figure 254. Loose bunch.	Frontal	Ball
18.	Compound plane S. P. – straight straddle sit, arms down holding the ball, lean forward with the ball rolling around the body, return to the starting position. 20' Individual exercises	Figure 255. Loose bunch.	Frontal	Ball
19.	Sagittal plane S. P. – prone position - arms to the side, the ball is in the right hand, raise the chest upwards while rolling the ball underneath to the left hand, then return to the starting position. 20x Individual exercises	Figure 256. Loose bunch.	Frontal	Ball
III. DYNAMIC FLEXIBILITY EXERCISES.				
20.	Legs S. P. – basic position - the ball in the right hand, dynamic alternate straight leg raises with the ball passing underneath from the outside, alternately on the right and left side, after finishing the exercise return to the starting position. 20' Individual exercises	Figure 257. Loose bunch.	Frontal	Ball
21.	Legs S. P. – basic position - the ball in the right hand, dynamic alternate straight leg raises with the ball passing underneath from the inside, alternately on the right and	Figure 258. Loose bunch.	Frontal	Ball

	left, return to the starting position. 30' Individual exercises			
22.	Legs S. P. – basic position - arms forward holding the ball, alternate dynamic straight leg lifts touching the foot to the ball, after finishing the exercise return to the starting position. 30' Individual exercises	Figure 259. Loose bunch.	Frontal	Ball
IV. DYNAMIC EXERCISES PERFORMED WHILE RUNNING – FAST RUN, MULTIPLE JUMPS COMBINED WITH COORDINATION EXERCISES.				
23.	Shoulders Legs S. P. – basic position - each exerciser has a ball in his hands, exercisers divided into 4 queues A, B, C, D - the first exercisers from queues A and C perform a pass on the ground with the inner part of the foot to exercisers from queues B and D and move quickly to the ends of the opposite queues while circling the ball around the torso to the left at the height of the chest and simultaneously performing an A skip, exercisers from queues B and D after receiving the ball with the sole perform the same exercise, after finishing the exercise return to the starting position. 1,5' Individual exercises	Figure 260. Square in a queue arrangement.	Frontal	Ball
24.	Shoulders Legs S. P. – basic position - each exerciser has a ball in his hands, exercisers divided into 4 queues A, B, C, D - the first		Frontal	Ball

	exercisers from queues A and C perform passes on the ground with their laces to exercisers in queues B and D and move quickly to the ends of the opposite queues while circling the ball around the torso to the right at the height of the chest and simultaneously performing a B skip, those exercising from queues B and D after receiving the ball with the sole perform the same exercise, after finishing the exercise return to the starting position. 1,5' Individual exercises	Figure 261. Square in a queue arrangement.		
25.	Legs S. P. – basic position - A, B, C, D - the first exercisers of each queue perform exercises with the ball at high speed, on the A side they roll the ball with alternating soles of their feet by hoping from foot to foot, on the B side they dribble the ball with their laces using their dominant foot, on the C side they roll the ball with alternating soles of their feet by hoping from foot to foot moving backwards, on the D side they dribble the ball with their laces using their weaker foot, after the exercise they run to the end of the next queue, after finishing the exercise return to the starting position 2' Individual exercises	Figure 262. Square in a queue arrangement.	Frontal	Ball

133

	V. STATIC OR DYNAMIC FLEXIBILITY EXERCISES.			
26.	Legs S. P. – basic position - alternate forward lunges, rolling the ball with hands around the foot of the front leg, after finishing the exercise return to the starting position. 12x Individual exercises	Figure 263. Square in a queue arrangement.	Frontal	Ball
27.	Legs S. P. – straddle position - the ball on the ground, standing on the right leg, raise the left leg forward, place the heel on the ball, bend forwards and grasp the toes of the left foot with left hand and hold in this position 5 sec, do the same exercise for the right leg, after finishing the exercise return to the starting position. 6x Individual exercises	Figure 264. Loose bunch.	Frontal	Ball
28.	Legs S. P. – sitting straight, hands down holding the ball, roll the ball with hands on the ground around the body, after finishing the exercise return to the starting position. 12x Individual exercises	Figure 265. Loose bunch.	Frontal	Ball
29.	Legs S. P. – lying back - the ball on the ground, place the ball under the back at the height of the lumbar spine, hands to the side, we roll the ball from the lumbar spine to the cervical part and back with the help of the legs, after finishing the exercise return to the starting position. 30" Individual exercises	Figure 266. Loose bunch.	Frontal	Ball

	VI. SPECIAL TECHNIQUE EXERCISES PERFORMED IN MOVEMENT.				
30.	Legs S. P. – basic position - the first exerciser from each queue leads the ball with the inner part of the foot, laces, internal laces, laces, the technique changes on the signal of the instructor, after completing the exercise he runs to the end of the next queue, after finishing the exercise return to the starting position 2' Individual exercises		Figure 267. The star in queues.	Frontal	Ball
31.	Legs S. P. – basic position, 2x2 small game, we play two games. The first game - 1.5' (30" active rest - exercisers in twos juggle the ball). Second game - 1.5' (30" active rest – exercisers in twos juggle the ball), after finishing the exercise return to the starting position. 4' Binary exercises		Figure 268. Combined.	Frontal	Ball
32.	Legs S. P. – basic position, players matched in twos pass on the floor, half-height, high ball with any method of trapping, passes at different distances (short, medium and long) in regard to each other, after finishing the exercise return to the starting position. 2' Binary exercises		Figure 269. Loose bunch.	Individual	Ball

6.5. Scenario of a warm-up with a ball and elements of game tactics before training

\multicolumn{5}{	c	}{SCENARIO OF A WARM-UP WITH A BALL AND ELEMENTS OF GAME TACTICS BEFORE TRAINING}
\multicolumn{5}{	c	}{I. SLOW RUN EXERCISES – ARMS AND LEGS EXERCISES.}
No.	EXERCISES DRILLS TIME – NUMBER OF REPETITIONS DIVISION OF EXERCISERS	EXERCISE SETTING	FORMS OF DRIBBLING	TEACHING AIDS
1.	Shoulders S. P. – basic position - exercisers try to perform the exercise simultaneously from all 4 queues, divided according to their position (e.g. defenders), slow run while throwing the ball up and catching it with their hands, after finishing the exercise return to the starting position. 30' Combined	Figure 270. Queue.	Frontal	Ball
2.	Shoulders S. P. – basic position - exercisers try to perform the exercise simultaneously from all 4 queues, divided according to their position (e.g. defender), slow run, every 3 steps, dropping the ball from their hands and volleying it up with their laces, arm circles forwards and backwards, receiving the ball with the thigh, after finishing the exercise return to the starting position. 30' Combined	Figure 271. Queue.	Frontal	Ball

3.	Shoulders S. P. – basic position - exercisers try to perform the exercise simultaneously from all 4 queues, divided according to their position (e.g. defenders), slow run, every 3 steps, dropping the ball from their hands and volleying the ball up with a straight leg, arm circles forwards and backwards, receiving the ball with the thigh, after finishing the exercise return to the starting position. 30' Combined	Figure 272. Queue.	Frontal	Ball
4.	Shoulders S. P. – basic position - exercisers try to perform the exercise simultaneously from all 4 queues, divided according to their position (e.g. defender), slow run, every 3 steps, dropping the ball from their hands and volleying it up with their laces, drop down to push up position, one repetition, stand and receive the ball after a bounce in any chosen way, after finishing the exercise return to the starting position. 30' Combined	Figure 273. Queue.	Frontal	Ball
5.	Legs S. P. – basic position - exercisers try to perform the exercise simultaneously from all 4 queues, divided according to their position (e.g. defender), slow run, every 3 steps, dropping the ball from their hands and volleying it up with a straight	Figure 274. Queue.	Frontal	Ball

	leg, A skip, receiving the ball with their laces, returning to their queue dribbling with their laces, after finishing the exercise return to the starting position. 30' Combined			
6.	Legs S. P. – basic position - exercisers try to perform the exercise simultaneously from all 4 queues, divided according to their position (e.g. defender), slow run, every 3 steps, dropping the ball from their hands and volleying it up with a straight leg, B skip, receiving the ball with the chest, returning to their queue dribbling with their outer laces, after finishing the exercise return to the starting position. 30' Combined	Figure 275. Queue.	Frontal	Ball
7.	Legs S. P. – basic position - exercisers try to perform the exercise simultaneously from all 4 queues, divided according to their position (e.g. defender), slow run, every 3 steps, dropping the ball from their hands and volleying it up with a straight leg, alternating forward lunges, receiving the ball any way, return to their queue dribbling the ball with internal laces, after finishing the exercise return to the starting position. 30' Combined	Figure 276. Queue.	Frontal	Ball

8.	Legs S. P. – basic position - exercisers try to perform the exercise simultaneously from all 4 queues, divided according to their position (e.g. defenders), slow running, juggling with feet, returning to their queue by dribbling the ball with any method, after finishing the exercise returning to the starting position. 30' Combined	Figure 277. Queue.	Frontal	Ball
II. STATIC EXERCISES – BODY EXERCISES, ROTATIONS OF PARTICULAR JOINTS, ROTATING TOE TOUCHES ETC.				
9.	Sagittal plane S. P. – straddle position - exercisers try to perform the exercise simultaneously from all formations in the system (e.g. 1-4-4-2), exercises are conducted by the exerciser as indicated by the leader using a gesture and voice command, (leaders are changed during the exercises), arms up holding the ball, forward and backward bends at the hips, after finishing the exercise return to the starting position. 12x Combined	Figure 278. A line - pitch formation.	Frontal	Ball
10.	Frontal plane S. P. – straddle position - exercisers try to perform the exercise simultaneously from all formations in the system (e.g. 1-4-4-2), exercises are conducted by the exerciser as indicated by the leader using a gesture and voice command, (leaders are changed during the exercises), arms up holding the ball, alternate side leans, after finishing the	Figure 279. A line - pitch formation.	Frontal	Ball

	exercise return to the starting position. 15" Combined			
11.	Sagittal plane S. P. – cross-legged position - exercisers try to perform the exercise simultaneously from all formations in the system (e.g. 1-4-4-2), exercises are conducted by the exerciser as indicated by the leader using a gesture and voice command, (leaders are changed during the exercises), arms forward holding the ball, bend forwards touching the head to the feet, after finishing the exercise return to the starting position. 15x Combined	Figure 280. A line - pitch formation.	Frontal	Ball
12.	Transverse plane S. P. – straddle position - exercisers try to perform the exercise simultaneously from all formations in the system (e.g. 1-4-4-2), exercises are conducted by the exerciser as indicated by the leader using a gesture and voice command, (leaders are changed during the exercises), torso twists with the ball in hands, left and right, after finishing the exercise return to the starting position. 15" Combined	Figure 281. A line - pitch formation.	Frontal	Ball
13.	Sagittal plane S. P. – lying back - exercisers try to perform the exercise simultaneously from all formations in the system (e.g. 1-4-4-2), exercises are conducted by the exerciser as indicated by the leader using a		Frontal	Ball

	gesture and voice command, (leaders are changed during the exercises), arms up holding the ball with both hands, raise the torso and place the ball between the feet, return to the supine position and lift the legs to the head and place the ball in the hands, after finishing the exercise return to the starting position. 15x Combined	Figure 282. A line - pitch formation		
14.	Compound plane S. P. – sit straight - exercisers try to perform the exercise simultaneously from all formations in the system (e.g. 1-4-4-2), exercises are conducted by the exerciser as indicated by the leader using a gesture and voice command, (leaders are changed during the exercises), arms forward holding the ball with both hands, rotate the torso to the left and right touching the ground with the ball on each side, the same in the other direction, after finishing the exercise return to the starting position. 15" Combined	Figure 283. A line - pitch formation.	Frontal	Ball
15.	Sagittal plane S. P. – prone position - exercisers try to perform the exercise simultaneously from all formations in the system (e.g. 1-4-4-2), exercises are conducted by the exerciser as indicated by the leader using a gesture and voice command, (leaders are changed during the exercises), arms forward holding the ball with both	Figure 284. A line - pitch formation.	Frontal	Ball

	hands, raise the chest, after finishing the exercise return to the starting position. 20x Combined			
	III. DYNAMIC FLEXIBILITY EXERCISES.			
16.	Legs S. P. – basic position - exercisers perform flexibility-improving exercises, on the signal of the coach, they set up on the pitch in a specific system (e.g. 1-4-4-2), arms forward holding the ball with both hands, balancing on the right leg, raise the left leg up and down, the same exercise for the right leg, after finishing the exercise return to the starting position. 30' Combined	Figure 285. A line - pitch formation.	Frontal	Ball
17.	Legs S. P. – exercisers perform exercises to improve flexibility, on the signal of the coach position themselves on the pitch in a specific formation (e.g. 1-4-4-2), hands resting on the ball, alternately swing the right leg and left leg backwards, after finishing the exercise return to the starting position. 30' Combined	Figure 286. A line - pitch formation.	Frontal	Ball
18.	Legs S. P. – kneeling - exercisers perform exercises to improve flexibility, on the signal of the coach they set up on the pitch in a specific system (e.g. 1-4-4-2), arms up holding the ball with both hands, bend forwards and backwards at the hips, after finishing the	Figure 287. A line - pitch formation.	Frontal	Ball

	exercise return to the starting position. 30' Combined			
19.	Legs S. P. – lying down - exercisers perform exercises to improve flexibility, on the signal of the coach they position themselves on the pitch in a specific system (e.g. 1-4-4-2), straight arms hold the ball over the chest, alternately raise legs to touch the ball, after finishing the exercise return to the starting position. 30' Combined	Figure 288. A line - pitch formation.	Frontal	Ball
IV. DYNAMIC EXERCISES PERFORMED RUNNING – FAST RUN, MULTIPLE JUMPS COMBINED WITH COORDINATION EXERCISES.				
20.	Shoulders Legs S. P. – basic position - exercisers lined up in teams of four facing each other, one group of four performs exercises, while the others imitate it on the principle of mirror reflection, during the exercises the trainer changes the leaders; arm circles forwards and backwards, dribbling in various ways in any directions and after finishing the exercise return to the starting position. 1,5' Individual exercises	Figure 289. A line - pitch formation.	Frontal	Ball
21.	Shoulders Legs S. P. – basic position - exercisers lined up in teams of four facing each other, a group of four performs exercises, while the others imitate it on the principle of mirror reflection, during exercises	Figure 290. A line - pitch formation.	Frontal	Ball

	the trainer changes the leaders; circulating the ball around the head, hips and knees in any direction, after finishing the exercise return to the starting position. 1,5' Individual exercises			
22.	Shoulders Legs S. P. – basic position - exercisers lined up in teams of four facing each other, a group of four performs exercises, and the other imitates it on the principle of mirror reflection, during the exercises the trainer changes the leaders; two-foot jumps over the ball, one leg jumps forwards and backwards and to the left and right, after finishing the exercise return to the starting position. 1' Individual exercises	Figure 291. A line - pitch formation.	Frontal	Ball
V. DYNAMIC OR STATIC FLEXIBILITY EXERCISES.				
23.	Torso Legs S. P. – straddle position, back to back, arms up; simultaneously bend forwards and pass the ball to the hands of the partner between the legs, simultaneously straighten-up and pass the ball over the head, after finishing the exercise return to the starting position. 12x Binary exercises	Figure 292. A number of pitch formations.	Frontal	Ball

24.	Legs S. P. – straddle position, facing each other; bend forwards holding each other's shoulders, ball held between the heads of the exercisers, they simultaneously swing the right leg, then the left leg keeping the ball motionless, after finishing the exercise return to the starting position. 10xRL 10xLL Binary exercises	Figure 293. A number of pitch formations.	Frontal	Ball
25.	Legs S. P. – basic position - facing each other; one exerciser holds the ball in front of him at chest height, the other exerciser balancing on one leg, the other leg raised, moves above the ball from the right to the left side, then changes the leg, switch the exercisers, after finishing the exercise return to the starting position. 10xRL 10xLL Binary exercises	Figure 294. A number of pitch formations.	Frontal	Ball
VI. SPECIAL TECHNIQUE EXERCISES PERFORMED IN MOVEMENT.				
26.	Legs S. P. – basic position - exercisers perform special technique exercises, on the leader's signal they position themselves on the playing field in a specific system (e.g. 1-4-4-2); e.g. hitting the ball against the training wall, juggling the ball with legs and head, dribbling in various ways with changes of pace, rolling the ball with the sole, throw-ins, after finishing the	Figure 295. Loose bunch.	Frontal	Ball

	exercise returning to the starting position. 5' Individual exercises			
27.	Legs S. P. – basic position - exercisers perform special technique exercises in twos, at the leader's signal they position themselves on the field in a specific system (e.g. 1-4-4-2); e.g. passing the ball to a partner in various ways at greater and smaller distances, juggling balls with legs and head in twos, 1x1 dribbling, after finishing the exercise return to the starting position. 5' Binary exercises	Figure 296. Loose bunch.	Frontal	Ball

6.6. Combined warm-up scenario before training sessions

	COMBINED WARM-UP SCENARIO BEFORE TRAINING SESSIONS			
	I. SLOW RUN EXERCISES – ARMS AND LEGS EXERCISES.			
No.	EXERCISES DRILLS TIME – NUMBER OF REPETITIONS DIVISION OF EXERCISERS	EXERCISE SETTING	METHOD OF DRIBBLING	TEACHING AIDS
1.	Shoulders Legs S. P. – basic position - in two groups, the exercisers juggle the ball with their right foot in place; on the signal of the coach slow run forwards without the ball to a partner, perform standing push-up with their partner, then return to their spot and to the starting position. 1x	Figure 297. Queue. Exercisers are divided into two groups A, B set across from each other, every exerciser has a ball have a	Frontal	Ball

		Combined	ball which they use to perform specific exercises commanded by the leader and on the signal of the coach, groups A and B perform a run without the ball and in the middle of the field they perform specific binary exercises, then return to their place or in the place of a partner.		
2.		Shoulders Legs S. P. – basic position - in two groups, the exercisers juggle the ball with their left foot in place; on the signal of the coach slow run forwards without the ball to a partner, double handed jumping high-five, then return back to their spot and to the starting position. 1x Combined	Figure 298. Queue. Exercisers are divided into two groups A, B set across from each other, every exerciser has a ball which they use to perform specific exercises commanded by the leader and on the signal, groups A and B perform a run without the ball and in the middle of the field they perform specific binary exercises, then return to their place or in the place of a partner.	Frontal	Ball
3.		Shoulders Legs S. P. – basic position - in two groups, the exercisers juggle the ball alternately with their feet in place; on the signal of the coach slow run backwards without a ball to a partner, a quarter turn and tap the partner's shoulder, then return backwards to their spot and to the starting position.	Figure 299. Queue. Exercisers are divided into two groups A, B set across from each other, every exerciser has a ball which	Frontal	Ball

4.	1x Combined	they use to perform specific exercises commanded by the leader and on the signal, groups A and B perform a run without the ball and in the middle perform specific binary exercises, then return to their place or in the place of a partner.		
4.	Shoulders Legs S. P. – basic position - in two groups, the exercisers juggle the ball with their heads in place; on the signal of the coach they perform a side shuffle with lateral arm swings to the middle, pass their partner then return to their spot and to the starting position. 1x Combined	Figure 300. Queue. Exercisers are divided into two groups A, B across from each other, each exerciser has a ball which they use to perform specific exercises commanded by the leader and on the signal, groups A and B perform a run without the ball and in the middle perform specific binary exercises, then return to their place or in the place of a partner.	Frontal	Ball
5.	Shoulders Legs S. P. – basic position - in two groups, the exercisers juggle the ball with their feet and head in place; on the signal of the coach, they grapevine towards the middle, perform a back to back resistance exercise moving in a circle, then return to their spot and to the starting position. 1x Combined	Figure 301. Queue. Exercisers are divided into two groups A, B across from each other, every exerciser has a ball which they use to perform specific exercises commanded by the leader	Frontal	Ball

		and on the signal, groups A and B perform a run without the ball and in the middle perform specific binary exercises, then return to their place or in the place of a partner.		
6.	Shoulders Legs S. P. – basic position - in two groups the exercisers juggle the ball with their right foot - head - left foot in place; on signal of the coach they A skip to each other, sit straight then run to the partner's place and return to the starting position. 1x Combined	Figure 302. Queue. Exercisers are divided into two groups A, B across from each other, every exerciser has a ball which they use to perform specific exercises commanded by the leader and on the signal, groups A and B perform a run without the ball and in the middle perform specific binary exercises, then return to their place or in the place of a partner.	Frontal	Ball
7.	Shoulders Legs S. P. – basic position - in two groups the exercisers jump over the ball forwards and backwards; on the signal of the coach, they C skip to the middle, perform a jumping chest bump with their partner then run to their partner's place and return to the starting position. 1x Combined	Figure 303. Queue. Exercisers are divided into two groups A, B across from each other, every exerciser has a ball which they use to perform specific exercises commanded by the leader and on the signal, groups A and B perform a run without the ball and in the middle they perform specific binary	Frontal	Ball

		exercises, then return to their place or in the place of a partner.		
8.	Shoulders Legs S. P. – basic position - in two groups, the exercisers jump over the ball to the right and left; on the signal of the coach, they go to the middle by jumping with alternating forward movement of arms and legs (skier jumping jacks), then they return to their place backwards and to the starting position. 1x Combined	Figure 304. Queue. Exercisers are divided into two groups A, B set across from each other, every exerciser has a ball which they use to perform specific exercises given by the leader and on the signal, groups A and B perform a run without the ball and in the middle perform specific binary exercises, then return to their place or in the place of a partner.	Frontal	Ball

II. EXERCISES PERFORMED IN PLACE OR DURING A SLOW RUN – TORSO EXERCISES, ROTATIONS OF PARTICULAR JOINTS, ROTATING TOE TOUCHES.

9.	Shoulders Legs Compound plane S. P. – basic position - group A and B exercisers pass the ball with the inside of the foot and run after the ball, group C and D exercisers perform the binary exercise after passing the ball, arms forward holding the partner's hands, single turn in a circle, then return to the starting position. 2x Combined	Figure 305. Queue. Exercisers are divided into four groups A, B, C, D and lined up opposite each other in queues. Two groups, A and B, have a ball. Group A and B - red, after passing the ball with the inner part of the foot run after the ball, groups C and D - blue, after passing the ball perform exercises in pairs.	Frontal	Ball

10.	Shoulders Legs Sagittal plane S. P. – basic position - group A and B exercisers pass the ball with the inside of the foot and run after the ball, group C and D exercisers, after passing the ball, come to each other and perform 5 synchronous forward bends at the hips, then with arms forward, actively pressing against their partner's hands, side shuffle face to face, and return to the starting position. 2x Combined	Figure 306. Queue. Exercisers are divided into four groups A, B, C, D and lined up opposite each other in queues. Two groups A and B have a ball. Group A and B - red, after passing the ball with the inner part of the foot run after the ball, groups C and D - blue, after passing the ball perform exercises in pairs.	Frontal	Ball
11.	Shoulders Legs Frontal plane S. P. – basic position - group A and B exercisers pass the ball with the inner part of the foot and run after the ball, group C and D exercisers after passing the ball come to each other and perform 5 synchronous side bends at the hips, then synchronous side shuffle face to face with simultaneous lateral arm swings and return to the starting position. 2x Combined	Figure 307. Queue. Exercisers are divided into four groups A, B, C, D and lined up opposite each other in queues. Two groups A and B have a ball. Group A and B - red, after passing the ball with the inner part of the foot run after the ball, groups C and D - blue, after passing the ball perform exercises in pairs.	Frontal	Ball
12.	Shoulders Legs Transverse plane S. P. – basic position - group A and B exercisers pass the ball with the inside of the foot and run after the ball, group C and D exercisers after receiving a	Figure 308. Queue.	Frontal	Ball

	ball, pass the ball and come to each other and perform 5 synchronous torso rotations, followed by a binary exercise where one partner does a stationary exercise and the second circles around the partner and it repeats every 3 steps, then they return to the starting position. 2x Combined	Exercisers are divided into four groups A, B, C, D and lined up opposite each other in queues. Two groups A and B have a ball. Group A and B - red, after passing the ball with the inner part of the foot run after the ball, groups C and D - blue, after passing the ball perform exercises in pairs.		
13.	Shoulders Legs Compound plane S. P. – basic position - group A and B exercisers pass the ball with the inner part of the foot and run after the ball, group C and D exercisers after passing the ball come to each other and perform hip rotations synchronously, 5 to the right and 5 to the left, then alternating jumps over the partner - so called "leap-frog" and then return to the starting position. 2x Combined	Figure 309. Queue. Exercisers are divided into four groups A, B, C, D and lined up opposite each other in queues. Two groups A and B have a ball. Group A and B - red, after passing the ball with the inner part of the foot run after the ball, groups C and D - blue, after passing the ball perform exercises in doubles.	Frontal	Ball

14.	Shoulders Legs Sagittal plane S. P. – basic position - group A and B exercisers pass the ball with the inner part of the foot and run after the ball, group C and D exercisers after passing the ball come to each other and perform 6 forward bends holding each other's shoulders trying to deepen the stretch, then alternately pass between the legs of the partner and return to the starting position. 2x Combined	Figure 310. Queue. Exercisers are divided into four groups A, B, C, D and lined up opposite each other in queues. Two groups A and B have a ball. Group A and B - red, after passing the ball with the inner part of the foot run after the ball, groups C and D - blue, after passing the ball perform exercises in doubles.	Frontal	Ball
	III. DYNAMIC FLEXIBILITY EXERCISES.			
15.	Legs S. P. – basic position - the exerciser passes the ball with the inside of the laces, then follows the ball, performing two-foot jumps with alternating abductions of the right and left leg, and returns to the starting position. 2x Individual exercises	Figure 311. Triangle in a queue arrangement.	Frontal	Ball
16.	Legs S. P. – basic position - the exerciser passes the ball with the inside of the laces, then follows the ball, performing alternating forward leg kicks forward and returns to the starting position. 2x Individual exercises	Figure 312. Triangle in a queue arrangement.	Frontal	Ball

No.	Exercise	Figure	Formation	Equipment
17.	Legs S. P. – basic position - the exerciser passes the ball with the inside of the laces, then follows the ball, performing alternating forward leg lunges and returns to the starting position. 2x Individual exercises	Figure 313. Triangle in a queue arrangement.	Frontal	Ball
IV. DYNAMIC EXERCISES PERFORMED WHILE RUNNING – FAST RUN MULTI JUMPS COMBINED WITH COORDINATION EXERCISES.				
18.	Shoulders Legs S. P. – basic position - after passing the ball with the inner part of the foot, single leg forward jumps and return to the starting position. 1x Individual exercises	Figure 314. Queue. Exercisers lined up in queues facing each other pass the ball with different parts of the foot and perform individual exercises in a fast run.	Frontal	Ball
19.	Legs S. P. – basic position - after passing the ball with the inside of the laces, A skip forward and return to the starting position. 1x Individual exercises	Figure 315. Queue. Exercisers lined up in queues facing each other pass the ball with different parts of the foot and perform individual exercises in a fast run.	Frontal	Ball
20.	Legs S. P. – basic position - after passing the ball with the laces, A skip backwards and return to the starting position. 1x		Frontal	Ball

		Figure 316. Queue. Exercisers lined up in queues facing each other pass the ball with different parts of the foot and perform individual exercises in a fast run.		
21.	Legs S. P. – basic position - after passing the ball with the outside of the laces, C skip and return to the starting position. 1x	Figure 317. Queue. Exercises lined up in queues facing each other pass the ball with different parts of the foot and perform individual exercises in a fast run.	Frontal	Ball
22.	Legs S. P. – basic position - after passing the ball with the inner part of the foot, inwards facing shuffle and return to the starting position. 1x Individual exercises	Figure 318. Queue. Exercisers lined up in queues facing each other pass the ball with different parts of the foot and perform individual exercises in a fast run.	Frontal	Ball

23.	Legs S.P. – basic position - after passing the ball with the inside of the laces, inwards facing shuffle and return to the starting position. 1x Individual exercises	Figure 319. Queue. Exercisers lined up in queues facing each other pass the ball with different parts of the foot and perform individual exercises in a fast run.	Frontal	Ball
24.	Legs S. P. – basic position - after passing the ball with the laces, outwards facing shuffle and return to the starting position. 1x Individual exercises	Figure 320. Queue. Exercisers lined up in queues facing each other pass the ball with different parts of the foot and perform individual exercises in a fast run.	Frontal	Ball
25.	Legs S. P. – basic position - after passing the ball with the outside of the laces, short intense runs at 80% of maximum speed and return to the starting position. 1x Individual exercises	Figure 321. Queue. Exercisers lined up in queues facing each other pass the ball with different parts of the foot and perform individual exercises in a fast run.	Frontal	Ball

	V. DYNAMIC OR STATIC FLEXIBILITY EXERCISES.			
26.	Legs S. P. – a) tension: prone position, left leg bent at the knee and right hand holding the foot, while trying to straighten the left leg as much as possible [20s] b) relaxation [3s]. c) stretching: in the same position, bend the left leg at the knee and grasp the foot with the right hand, then strongly pull until the heel touches the buttocks [20s] 1x LL & RL Individual exercises	Figure 322. Circle.	Frontal	Lack
27.	Legs S. P. – a) tension: in a basic position, arms forward with slightly bent knees -so-called "Slalom position" [20s]. b) relaxation [3s]. c) stretching: in the basic position, forward bend at the hips, grab the lower leg with the hands as low as possible and hold in this position [20s]. 1x Individual exercises	Figure 323. Circle.	Frontal	Lack
28.	Legs S. P. – a) tension: basic position, lunge forward, hands on the knee of the bent leg, other leg pressed back as hard as possible against the floor [20s]. b) relaxation [3s]. c) stretching: basic position, lunge forward, torso straight, trying to push the hips as far forward as possible and staying in this position [20s]. 1x Individual exercises	Figure 324. Circle.	Frontal	Lack

	VI. SPECIAL TECHNIQUE EXERCISES PERFORMED IN MOVEMENT WITH A BALL AND COORDINATION EXERCISES WITH ACCESSORIES e.g. COORDINATION LADDER, COORDINATION PLATFORM.			
29.	Shoulders Legs S. P. – basic position, 5x5 small game, play two games. The first game - 3 '(2' active rest - practicing special technique exercises in twos, e.g. passing the ball to a partner in various ways with greater and smaller distances, juggling the ball in pairs with feet and head, dribbling 1x1). Second game - 3 ', (2' active rest), return to the starting position. 1' Combined	Figure 325. Combined.	Frontal	Ball

6.7. Goalkeeper warm-up scenario before training

	GOALKEEPER WARM-UP SCENARIO BEFORE TRAINING			
	I. SLOW RUN EXERCISES – ARMS AND LEGS EXERCISES.			
No.	EXERCISES DRILLS TIME – NUMBER OF REPETITIONS DIVISION OF EXERCISERS	EXERCISE SETTING	METHOD OF LEADING	TEACHING AIDS
1.	Legs S. P. – basic position – forward shuffle then jog back to the starting position. 2x Individual exercises	Figure 326. Queue.	Frontal	None
2.	Legs S. P. – basic position – forward shuffle and then a jump then jog back to the starting position. 2x Individual exercises	Figure 327. Queue.	Frontal	None
3.	Legs		Frontal	None

	S. P. – basic position – grapevine then jog back to the starting position. 2x Individual exercises	Figure 328. Queue.		
4.	Legs S. P. – basic position - run, squat and jump up every 3 steps then jog back to the starting position forward. 2x Individual exercises	Figure 329. Queue.	Frontal	None
5.	Shoulders S. P. – basic position - forward run, forward arm circles then jog back to the starting position. 2x Individual exercises	Figure 330. Queue.	Frontal	None
6.	Shoulders S. P. – basic position – backwards run, backward arm circles then jog back to the starting position. 2x Individual exercises	Figure 331. Queue.	Frontal	None
7.	Shoulders S. P. – basic position – backwards run, alternating upward arm swings then jog back to the starting position. 2x Individual exercises	Figure 332. Queue.	Frontal	None
8.	Shoulders Legs S. P. – basic position - forward run, every 3 steps a single jumping jack with a 360° rotation, then jog back to the starting position. 2x Individual exercises	Figure 333. Queue.	Frontal	None

9.	Shoulders Legs S. P. – basic position – backwards run, every 3 steps simultaneous forward arm circles while jumping counting to 5 then jog back to the starting position. 2x Individual exercises	Figure 334. Queue.	Frontal	None
II. STATIONARY EXERCISES – BODY EXERCISES, ROTATIONS OF PARTICULAR JOINTS, ROTATING TOE TOUCHES.				
10.	Sagittal plane S. P. – basic position - arms up with the ball held in both hands, forward bend at the hips until the ball touches the ground, then return to the starting position. 10x Individual exercises	Figure 335. Loose bunch.	Frontal	Ball
11.	Sagittal plane S. P. – basic position - arms down holding the ball in both hands, throwing the ball up and catching it behind the back, then return to the starting position. 10x Individual exercises	Figure 336. Loose bunch.	Frontal	Ball
12.	Sagittal plane S. P. – basic position - arms behind the back holding the ball with both hands, throw the ball up and catch it in front, then return to the starting position. 10x Individual exercises	Figure 337. Loose bunch.	Frontal	Ball
13.	Transverse plane S. P. – basic position - arms forward holding the ball in both hands, torso rotations to the right and left, then return to the starting position. 15' Individual exercises	Figure 338. Loose bunch.	Frontal	Ball

14.	Compound plane S. P. – straddle position - arms down holding the ball, forward bend at the hips, rolling the ball on the ground in figure-eights around the right leg and left leg, then return to the starting position. 20' Individual exercises	Figure 339. Loose bunch.	Frontal	Ball
15.	Compound plane S. P. – straight sit - the ball between the legs, transition from straight sit to supine position with legs lifted as far as the head and passing the ball from the legs to the hands and back, then return to the starting position. 15x Individual exercises	Figure 340. Loose bunch.	Frontal	Ball
16.	Compound plane S. P. – straight sit - hands down holding the ball, throws of the ball up and to the right and left, alternately, catch the ball after the bounce, then return to the starting position. 10x right side 10x left side Individual exercises	Figure 341. Loose bunch.	Frontal	Ball
	III. DYNAMIC FLEXIBILITY EXERCISES.			
17.	Legs S. P. – basic position - extensive alternating legs swings forwards and backwards, then return to the starting position. 10xRl 10xLl Individual exercises	Figure 342. Loose bunch.	Frontal	None
18.	Legs S. P. – basic position – forward bend, hands touching the ground, straighten up, and raise the arms above the head, then return to the starting position. 15x	Figure 343. Loose bunch.	Frontal	None

	Individual exercises			
19.	Legs S. P. – basic position - squat, hands on the hips, alternate extensions of the legs to the side lifting the foot up off of the ground, at the same time deepening the squat, then return to the starting position. 15x Individual exercises	Figure 344. Loose bunch.	Frontal	None
20.	Shoulders Legs S. P. – basic position - squat with the hands on the ground, from this position jump up straightening the whole body, forcefully throwing the arms up to help, then return to the starting position. 10x Individual exercises	Figure 345. Loose bunch.	Frontal	None
21.	Shoulders Legs S. P. – straddle position - maximum extension of the arms above the head, squat and drop the arms with a swing backwards, then return to the starting position. 10x Individual exercises	Figure 346. Loose bunch	Frontal	None
IV. GYMNASTIC EXERCISES PERFORMED WITHOUT A BALL.				
22.	Shoulders S. P. – four-point kneeling (plank position) on the forearms; rolling sideways, then return to the starting position. 5x right side 5x left side Individual exercises	Figure 347. Loose bunch.	Frontal	None

23.	Shoulders Legs S. P. – squat with hands on the ground; forward somersault, then return to the starting position. 10' Individual exercises	Figure 348. Loose bunch.		Frontal	None
24.	Shoulders Legs S. P. – squat with hands on the ground; backwards somersault, then return to the starting position. 10' Individual exercises	Figure 349. Loose bunch.		Frontal	None
25.	Shoulders Legs S. P. squat with hands on the ground; backwards somersault from straddle position to straddle position, then return to the starting position. 10' Individual exercises	Figure 350. Loose bunch.		Frontal	None
26.	Shoulders Legs S. P. – basic position; slow running, somersault forward, then return to the starting position. 5x Individual exercises	Figure 351. Loose bunch.		Frontal	None
27.	Shoulders Legs S. P. – basic position; handstand, then return to the starting position. 5x Individual exercises	Figure 352. Loose bunch.		Frontal	None
28.	Shoulders Legs S. P. – basic position; onto all fours, fall forward to the stomach with the arms bent and elbows against the body, then return to the starting position.	Figure 353. Loose bunch.		Frontal	None

	5x Individual exercises			
29.	Shoulders Legs S. P. – in supine position, bringing the legs past the head, then return to the starting position. 8x Individual exercises	Figure 354. Loose bunch.	Frontal	None
30.	Shoulders Legs S. P. – basic position; half-squat, hands on the ground and kick the legs back simultaneously into a plank position (hare jumps with marking the flight phase - burpees), then return to the starting position. 5x Individual exercises	Figure 355. Loose bunch.	Frontal	None
31.	Shoulders Legs S. P. – basic position; half-squat, dive forward, then return to the starting position. 5x Individual exercises	Figure 356. Loose bunch.	Frontal	None
V. DYNAMIC OR STATIC FLEXIBILITY EXERCISES.				
32.	Legs S. P. – basic position - arms down with the ball held in both hands, high alternate leg raises with the ball being moved once under the right leg, once the left leg, then return to the starting position. 10x RL 10x LL Individual exercises	Figure 357. Loose bunch.	Frontal	Ball
33.	Legs S. P. – straddle position - arms up with the ball held in both hands, bend forward at the hips with the ball touching the		Frontal	Ball

	ground in front of the feet once on the right and once on the left, then return to the starting position. 10x RL 10x LL Individual exercises	Figure 358. Loose bunch.		
34.	Legs S. P. – basic position - arms sideways bent with the ball held in both hands, walking in-place with high knees that touch the ball, after finishing the exercise return to the starting position. 10x PN 10x LN Individual exercises	Figure 359. Loose bunch.	Frontal	Ball
35.	Shoulders S. P. – basic position - arms up with the ball held in both hands, bend backwards at the hips then throw the ball against the ground in front and catch the ball, then return to the starting position. 15x Individual exercises	Figure 360. Loose bunch.	Frontal	Ball
VI. GYMNASTIC EXERCISES PERFORMED WITH A BALL.				
36.	Shoulders Legs S. P. – basic position, throw the ball up, somersault forward, stand and catch the ball in the air, then return to the starting position. 5x Individual exercises	Figure 361. Loose bunch.	Frontal	Ball
37.	Shoulders Legs S. P. – basic position, throw the ball up, somersault backwards, stand and catch the ball in the air, then return to the starting position. 5x Individual exercises	Figure 362. Loose bunch.	Frontal	Ball

38.	Shoulders Legs S. P. – basic position, throw the ball up, dive forward, quickly stand up and catch the ball in the air, then return to the starting position. 5x Individual exercises	Figure 363. Loose bunch.	Frontal	Ball
39.	Shoulders Legs S. P. – basic position, throw the ball up, lie down, quickly stand up and catch the ball in the air, then return to the starting position. 5x Individual exercises	Figure 364. Loose bunch.	Frontal	Ball
40.	Shoulders Legs S. P. – basic position, throw the ball up, lie down, stand and catch the ball after a bounce, then return to the starting position. 5x Individual exercises	Figure 365. Loose bunch.	Frontal	Ball
41.	Shoulders Legs S. P. – basic position, throw the ball up, dive forwards, stand up and catch the ball after a bounce, then return to the starting position. 5x Individual exercises	Figure 366. Loose bunch.	Frontal	Ball
42.	Shoulders Legs S. P. – straddle sit, players pass two balls simultaneously with a transition to a sideways dive, then return to the starting position. 20' Binary exercises	Figure 367. Loose bunch.	Frontal	Ball

43.	Shoulders Legs S. P. – basic position, player A throws the ball over player B, who straddle jumps and catches the ball in the air, then return to the starting position. 5x Binary exercises	Figure 368. Loose bunch.	Frontal	Ball
44.	Shoulders Legs S. P. – basic position, player A, crouching position, hands on the legs, player B straddle jumps over his partner, crawls between his legs and catches the ball shot at him, then return to the starting position. 5x Binary exercises	Figure 369. Loose bunch.	Frontal	Ball

I would like to thank you for using this vade mecum, I hope you found it useful.
It was also a pleasure to write this book and cooperate with Marcin Oślizło. I hope that we will write another useful book soon.
Special thanks to other authors, for the support and motivation. I also can't forget about my family who had to put up with me during this difficult time, I love you.

Robert Makuch

BIBLIOGRAPHY

1. **Abade E, Sampaio J, Gonçalves B, Baptista J, Alves A, Viana J.** Effects of different re-warm up activities in football players' performance. PLoS One., 2017 Jun 29; 12(6): e0180152.
2. **Barengo NC, Meneses-Echávez JF, Ramírez-Vélez R, Cohen DD, Tovar G, Bautista JE.** The impact of the FIFA 11+ training program on injury prevention in football players: a systematic review. Int J Environ Res Public Health., 2014; 11: 1986–2000.
3. **Beale M.** The Ultimate Soccer Warm-Ups Manual. Soccer Coach; 2007, p. 106.
4. **Beale M.** The Ultimate Soccer Warm-Ups Manual: 126 Quick and Easy Ways to Kick-off Your Coaching Sessions 2015. Green Star Media; 2015, p. 190.
5. **Bergier J, Buraczewski T.** Wzorce symetrii techniki strzałów i podań w piłce nożnej w mistrzostwach świata 2002. In: Nowoczesna gra w piłkę nożną – teoria i praktyka, (ed.) A. Stuła, Wydawnictwo „OSGRAF", Gorzów Wielkopolski, 2003; 69–75.
6. **Bischops K, Gerards H.** Piłka nożna – rozgrzewka. Wydawnictwo: Marshal; 1999.
7. **Bizzini M, Junge A, Dvorak J.** Implementation of the FIFA 11+ football warm up program: how to approach and convince the Football associations to invest in prevention. Br J Sports Med., 2013; 47: 803–806.
8. **Bizzini M, Impellizzeri FM, Dvorak J, Bortolan L, Schena F, Modena R, Junge A.** Physiological and performance responses to the "FIFA 11+" (part 1): is it an appropriate warm-up? J Sports Sci., 2013; 31(13): 1481-1490.
9. **Bizzini M, Eiles M, Fulcher M, Haratian Z, Dvorak J.** Injury prevention in football and FIFA 11+. A model for International Sports Federations? Aspetar Journal, 2016; 5: 42-49.
10. **Bompa T.** Przygotowanie sprawnościowe w zespołowych grach sportowych. Wydawnictwo AWF Katowice; 2013.
11. **Chmura J., Jung K.** Wpływ wysiłku wytrzymałościowo – szybkościowego na przebieg zmian sprawności psychomotorycznej piłkarzy. Sport Wyczynowy, 1992; 7/8: 24-35.
12. **Chmura J, Nazar K, Kościuba-Uściłko H.** Choice reaction time during graded exercise In relation to blond lactate and plasma catecholamine thershold. International Jurnal of Sports Medicine, 1994; 15(4): 172-176.
13. **Chmura J, Krysztofiak H, Ziemba A, Nazar K, Kaciuba-Uściłko H.** Psychomotor performance during prolonged exercise above and below the blood lac-tate threshold. European Journal of Applied Physiology and Occupational Physiology, 1998; 77: 77-80.
14. **Chmura J.** Szybkość działania zawodnika w piłce nożnej. Wydanie specjalne: Trener piłki nożnej – wybrane zagadnienia z teorii i praktyki treningu sportowego. Medicina Sportiva, 2004; Vol. 8, Suppl. 1, AWF Kraków: 75-96.
15. **Chmura J.** Rozgrzewka – podstawy fizjologiczne i zastosowanie praktyczne. Wydawnictwo Lekarskie: PZWL; 2014.

16. **Chmura J.** Szybkość w piłce nożnej. Wydawnictwo: AWF Katowice; 2014.
17. **Cicirko L.** Ogólnie o rozgrzewce piłkarskiej. Trener, 2004; 1: 12-16.
18. **Czubaj M., Drozda J., Myszkorowski J.** Postfutbol – antropologia piłki nożnej. Wydawnictwo Naukowe: Katedra; 2012.
19. **Doktór K., Talaga J., Pilkiewicz M.** Piłka nożna początku XXI wieku w świetle obserwacji i analiz XVII Mistrzostw Świata Korea/Japonia 2002. Sport Wyczynowy, 2002; 7/8: 83-99.
20. **Duda H.** Intelektualizacja nauczania gry w piłkę nożną. Wydawnictwo: AWF Kraków; 2004a.
21. **Duda H.** EURO' 2004 – analiza działań ofensywnych najlepszych zespołów. Sport Wyczynowy, 2004b; 11/12: 9-15.
22. **Duda H.** Intelektualizacja w szkoleniu technicznym piłkarza. In: Podstawy racjonalnego szkolenia w grze w piłkę nożną, (ed.) S. Żak, H. Duda, Wydawnictwo AWF, Kraków, 2006a; 109–130.
23. **Duda H.** Jak Europa gra w piłkę nożną? Analiza sytuacji bramkowych w ME Portugalia 2004. Sport Wyczynowy, 2006b; 5/6: 13-22.
24. **Duda H.** Intelektualizacja procesu nauczania, a rozwój dyspozycji do gry zespołowej (na przykładzie piłki nożnej). Wydawnictwo: Studia i monografie nr 50, AWF Kraków; 2008.
25. **Duda H., Basiaga-Pasternak J.** Wpływ świadomej analizy zadania ruchowego na skuteczność działania piłkarzy nożnych. In: Teoretyczne i praktyczne aspekty nowoczesnej gry w piłkę nożną, (ed.) A. Stuła, Wydawnictwo Politechnika Opolska", 2009; 33–48.
26. **Fajfer Z.** Wyszukiwanie, wspomaganie i wybór utalentowanej młodzieży grającej w piłkę nożną w Republice Czech. In: Nowoczesna gra w piłkę nożną – teoria i praktyka, (ed.) A. Stuła, Wydawnictwo „OSGRAF", Gorzów Wielkopolski, 2003; 43–52.
27. **Friedrich C.** 750+ Soccer Drills: Warm Up & Skill Building: Soccer Football Practice Drills For Youth Coaching & Skills Training: Volume 1 (Youth Soccer Coaching Drills Guide). CreateSpace Independent Publishing Platform; 2015, p. 780.
28. **Gerards N.** Warm up in football: training sessions y matches. Green Star Media; 2017, p. 190.
29. **Gołaszewski J.** Piłka nożna. Wydawnictwo: AWF Poznań; 2003.
30. **Grooms DR, Palmer T, Onate JA, Myer GD, Grindstaff T.** Soccer-specific warm-up and lower extremity injury rates in collegiate male soccer players. J Athl Train., 2013; 48: 782–789.
31. **Grycman P., Szyngiera W.:** Nowoczesne nauczanie i doskonalenie gry w pikę nożną. Wydawnictwo: Grycman Paweł; 2016.
32. **Hammami A, Zois J, Slimani M, Russel M, Bouhlel E.** The efficacy and characteristics of warm-up and re-warm-up practices in soccer players: a systematic review. J Sports Med Phys Fitness., 2018 Jan-Feb; 58(1-2): 135-149.

33. **Impellizzeri FM, Bizzini M, Dvorak J, Pellegrini B, Schena F, Junge A.** Physiological and performance responses to the FIFA 11+ (part 2): a randomised controlled trial on the training effects. J Sports Sci., 2013; 31(13): 1491-1502.
34. **James C.** Warm Up Drills for Soccer: Fun Warm Ups with and without a Ball. Reedswain Incorporated; 2004, p. 149.
35. **Jastrzębski Z., Szwarc A.** Struktura organizacyjna i jej wpływ na efektywność szkolenia piłkarskiego na przykładzie Szkoły Mistrzostwa Sportowego w Gdańsku. Wydawnictwo: AWF Gdańsk; 2003.
36. **Kirkendall D.** Anatomia w piłce nożnej. Wydawnictwo: Muza; 2012.
37. **Kubica R.** Podstawy fizjologii pracy i wydolności fizycznej. Wydawnictwo: Skrypt AWF Katowice; 1995.
38. **Kucharczyk A.** Jak rozwijać inteligentnych piłkarzy? Trener, 2013; 5: 18-21.
39. **Kuczma K.** Ciekawa historia piłkarskich mistrzostw świata. Sport Wyczynowy, 2010; 3/4: 7-33.
40. **Loy R.** Schuss mit den Aufwarmiten vor dem spiel.. Fusballtraining, 2000; 11-12: 18-21.
41. **Lucchesi M.** Soccer tactics an analysis of attack & defence. Reedswain; 2000.
42. **Martin J.** The best of soccer journal: technique & tactics. Meyer & Meyer; 2012.
43. **Martín-García A, Gómez Díaz A, Bradley PS, Morera F, Casamichana D.** Quantification of a Professional Football Team's External Load Using a Microcycle Structure. J Strength Cond Res., 2018 Dec; 32(12): 3511-3518.
44. **Mayo M., Seijas R., Alvarez P.** Structured neuromuscular warm-up for injury prevention in young elite football players. Rev Esp Cir Ortop Traumatol., 2014 Nov-Dec; 58(6): 336-342.
45. **Naglak Z.** Zespołowa gra sportowa. Studium. Wydawnictwo: Studia i monografie nr 45, AWF Wrocław; 1994.
46. **Naglak Z.** Teoria zespołowej gry sportowej – kształcenie gracza. Wydawnictwo: AWF Wrocław; 2001.
47. **Naglak Z.** Nauczanie i uczenie się wielopodmiotowej gry w piłkę – kształcenia gracza na wstępnym etapie. Wydawnictwo: AWF Wrocław; 2005.
48. **Nosal J.** Poziomy kontroli i oceny sprawności zawodnika w przygotowaniu do gry w piłkę nożną. In: Nowoczesna piłka nożna – teoria i praktyka, (ed.) A. Stuła, Wydawnictwo P.W. „OPEN", Gorzów Wielkopolski", 1999; 99–112.
49. **Owoeye OB, Akinbo SR, Tella BA, Olawale OA.** Efficacy of the FIFA 11+ Warm-Up Programme in Male Youth Football: a cluster randomised controlled trial. J Sports Sci Med., 2014; 13: 321–328.
50. **Panfil R., Żmuda W.** Nauczanie gry w piłkę nożną. Wydawnictwo: BK; 1999.
51. **Panfil R., Paluszek K.** Kryteria procesu edukacji sportowca z uzdolnieniami do gry w piłkę nożną. In: Nowoczesna gra w piłkę nożną – teoria i praktyka, (ed.) A. Stuła, Wydawnictwo „OSGRAF", Gorzów Wielkopolski, 2003; 7–20.
52. **Rössler R, Verhagen E, Rommers N, Dvorak J, Junge A, Lichtenstein E, Donath L, Faude O.** Comparison of the '11+ Kids' injury prevention programme and a

regular warmup in children's football (soccer): a cost effectiveness analysis. Br J Sports Med., 2019; Mar; 53(5): 309-314.

53. **Sardar B, Verma K.** Effect of Warm-Up on Selected Soccer Skill Performance: Warm-Up and Soccer Skill Performance. LAP LAMBERT: Academic Publishing; 2014, p. 64.

54. **Silva LM, Neiva HP, Marques MC, Izquierdo M, Marinho DA.** Effects of Warm-Up, Post-Warm-Up, and Re-Warm-Up Strategies on Explosive Efforts in Team Sports: A Systematic Review. Sports Med., 2018 Oct; 48(10): 2285-2299.

55. **Silvers H, Mandelbaum BR, Adeniji O, Insler S, Bizzini M, Pohlig R, Junge A, Snyder-Mackler L, Dvorak J.** The efficacy of the FIFA 11+ program in the Collegiate Male Soccer Players. Am J Sports Med., 2015 Nov; 43(11): 2628-2637.

56. **Spurrier D.** Critically appraised paper: The 11+ Kids' warm-up program performed at least once a week reduces severe and lower extremity injuries in children playing football [commentary]. J Physiother., 2019; Jan; 65(1): 53. doi: 10.1016/j.jphys.2018.10.001.

57. **Steffen K, Emery CA, Romiti M, Kang J, Bizzini M, Dvorak J, Finch CF, Meeuwisse WH.** High adherence to a neuromuscular injury prevention programme (FIFA 11+) improves functional balance and reduces injury risk in Canadian youth female football players: a cluster randomised trial. Br J Sports Med., 2013; 47: 794–802.

58. **Steffen K, Emery CA, Romiti M, Kang J, Bizzini M, Dvorak J, Finch CF, Meeuwisse WH.** High adherence to a neuromuscular injury prevention programme (FIFA 11+) improves functional balance and reduces injury risk in Canadian youth female football players: a cluster randomised trial. Br J Sports Med., 2013; 47: 794–802.

59. **Stępiński M.** Taktyka współczesnej piłki nożnej. Wydawnictwo: Zysk i S-ka; 2007.

60. **Stępiński M.** Materiały pomocnicze do przedmiotu piłka nożna dla studentów IKF US. Wydawnictwo Naukowe: Uniwersytetu Szczecińskiego; 2009.

61. **Stuła A.** Skuteczność wybranych elementów gry najlepszych zespołów piłkarskich Mistrzostw Europy Anglia'96. Sport Wyczynowy, 1998; 5/6: 28-47.

62. **Szwarc A.** Metody oceny techniczno – taktycznych działań piłkarzy nożnych. Wydawnictwo: AWFiS Gdańsk; 2003.

63. **Szwarc A, Piątek M.** Charakterystyka gry w piłkę nożną. In: Vademecum piłki nożnej, (ed.) A. Szwarc, Wydawnictwo AWF Gdańsk, 2010; 9-28.

64. **Talaga J.** Taktyka piłki nożnej. Wydawca: Biblioteka Trenera, RCMSzFKiS; 1997.

65. **Talaga J.** ABC młodego piłkarza – nauczanie techniki. Wydawnictwo: Zysk i S-ka; 2006a.

66. **Talaga J.** Mundialowe refleksje. Sport Wyczynowy, 2006b; 5/6: 7-12.

67. **Talaga J.** Rozwojowe treści rozgrzewki piłkarza – część 1. Trener, 2008; 6: 27-35.

68. **Talaga J.** Rozwojowe treści rozgrzewki piłkarza – część 2. Trener, 2009; 1: 29-37.

69. **Tyka A.** Wpływ stosowania zróżnicowanej rozgrzewki na zdolność organizmu do pracy krótkotrwałej o maksymalnej mocy. Wydawnictwo: AWF Kraków, 1995.

70. **Verheijen R.** Periodisation in football: Preparing the Korean national team for the 2002 World Cup. Insight: The FA Coaches Association Journal, 2003; 6 (2): 30-33.
71. **Wagner W, Rumak M.** Regresja liniowa segmentacyjna skuteczności strzelonych bramek w piłce nożnej. In: Współczesna piłka nożna – teoria i praktyka, (ed.) A. Stuła, P.W. „OPEN" Gorzów Wielkopolski, 2001; 63-68.
72. **Wilson J.** Inverting the Pyramid: The History of Football Tactics. Orion; 2009.
73. **Wrzos J.** Piłkarska reprezentacja Polski na tle europejskiej i światowej elity. Sport Wyczynowy, 2005; 3/4: 28-47.
74. **Żak S, Duda H.** Podstawy racjonalnego szkolenia w grze w piłkę nożną. Wydawnictwo: AWF Kraków; 2006.
75. **Żmuda W.** Ocena i kontrola poziomu umiejętności techniczno – taktycznych piłkarzy. In: Diagnostyka przygotowania zawodników do gry w piłce nożnej, (ed.) I. Ryguła. AWF, Katowice, 1998; 167-202.
76. **Żmuda W.** Tendencje rozwojowe piłki nożnej na podstawie analizy ME - 2000. In: Współczesna piłka nożna – teoria i praktyka, (ed.) A. Stuła, P.W. „OPEN", Gorzów Wielkopolski, 2001; 125-140.
77. **Żmuda W, Szyngiera W, Góralczyk R.** Analiza porównawcza mistrzostw świata (1990-1998) jako wykładnik tendencji rozwojowych w piłce nożnej. In: Nowoczesna piłka nożna – teoria i praktyka, (ed.) A. Stuła, P.W. „OPEN", Gorzów Wielkopolski, 1999; 125-134.

Bei Fragen zur Produktsicherheit wenden Sie sich bitte an:
If you have any questions regarding product safety,
please contact:

Walter de Gruyter GmbH
Genthiner Straße 13
10785 Berlin
productsafety@degruyterbrill.com